MERRILY ON HIGH

COLIN STEPHENSON

CANTERBURY
PRESS
Norwich

FOR JOHN AND BETTY ROBEY

Also by the same author and published by Canterbury Press in 2008
Walsingham Way

© Colin Stephenson 1972, 2008

First published in 1972 by Darton, Longman & Todd.
This edition published in 2008 by the Canterbury Press Norwich
(a publishing imprint of Hymns Ancient & Modern Limited,
a registered charity)
Editorial office: 13–17 Long Lane, London EC1A 9PN
Second Impression 2010

www.scm-canterburypress.co.uk

British Library Cataloguing in Publication data

A catalogue record for this book is available
from the British Library

ISBN 978-1-85311-912-5

Printed in the UK by CPI William Clowes
Beccles, NR34 7TL

Contents

Preface to the Second Edition

Colin Stephenson was the best raconteur I ever met. Whether one was alone with him or in a big crowd, he never failed to produce a constant stream of wildly funny stories or shrewd comments on people and ideas. Only the sight of good food could halt him in his tracks. I well remember him at the end of a large meal in an Edinburgh restaurant, stopping just before the punch-line of a particularly wild tale, to watch wistfully as a waiter went by with a heaped tray of food. Not till he was out of sight did Colin produce the hilarious end to the story. The occasion was the funnier because he was playing truant from an expensive health spa where friends had persuaded him to go with them to reduce his weight!

As *Merrily on High* shows, Colin was a mixture of a genuine lover of the Church, with all its disciplines, and a delightful lover of God's creation, with all its beauties. In his company people felt more of a zest for life and, when they knew him better, they came to realize that this zest was accompanied by a deep love of God and his neighbour and a genuine humility. G.K. Chesterton said, 'The humble man will always be talkative; for he is interested in his subject and knows that it is best shown in talk.' Although *Merrily on High* is a 'churchy' autobiography, it is not introspective: Colin's interest was in other people, not in himself.

The poet John Betjeman told Colin that when he received his copy of *Merrily on High* he took it to read on a train journey. He confessed that he had laughed so much that his fellow passengers almost called the guard to have him removed! Of course Betjeman shared Colin's love of the Church of England and especially its

Catholic wing and the eccentric people who were among the inhabitants of that wing in Colin's day. Colin had a genius for finding just the right word or the right tone of voice that conveyed the absurdity and fun of growing up in the days of Anglo-Catholic triumphalism.

He was a great drawer of word-pictures. For example:

Along the sides (of St Bartholomew's, Brighton) were confessional boxes which seemed as if the Royal Pavilion had had puppies.

When I was priested, the headmistress of the Infant School said to the children, 'You can now call Father "Father" and mean it because he really is a Father now. They looked at me with innocent eyes, but some of them were more sophisticated than she thought and one little cherub came up to me afterwards and said, 'Who had the baby?

(In St Magnus the Martyr) a lot of old ladies, many wearing blue veils, were responding '*ora pro nobis*' to the Litany of the Saints. As I entered, Fynes-Clinton had just said, '*Omnes sancti angeli et arcangeli*', and all the women shouted, '*Ora pro nobis.*' A reproachful face turned from the altar and said reprovingly, '*Orate pro nobis.*'

Colin loved this side of the Church of England even though he lived long enough to see the results of the Second Vatican Council on much of Anglo-Catholicism. In his latter years as a sort of private Chaplain at Souh Park, the home of Mel and Uvedale Lambert, he said Mass daily, as he had always done, but there wasn't a biretta or maniple in sight. In a way, Colin's total immersion in the Papalist end of the C of E caused him to abandon much of the outward signs of the Catholic faith, because this was what was happening in the Roman Catholic Church. When asked about his view on authority in the Church, he said, 'I find any theory of authority which by-passes the Bishop of Rome less than satisfactory.' But then, in typical Colin fashion he added, 'When Bishop Wand published a book entitled *What the Church of England Stands For*, a wag said to me, "The answer to that is, 'because there is only one seat and the Pope's in it!'"'

It is interesting to speculate what Colin would now make of a Pope who is gently nudging the Church back to the fullness of the old Rite. This cannot be answered now that he is 'merrily on high', but I think he may be having a gentle laugh. In the end, his entire ministry, and the charm and value of this book, can be summed up in what he says in Chapter 6, 'I very much enjoyed parish work because I am fortunate enough to like people', and he liked them colourful like the Catholic Faith in all its glory. He did not despise 'middle-stump Anglicanism' or Evangelicals, but it was not for him. As he said, 'I did once go into a low church and the clergyman who was standing at the door said, "Dull, isn't it?" I agreed heartily till I discovered he was talking about the weather!'

Gordon Reid
Philadelphia
July 2008

Foreword

THE MOST UNEVENTFUL life produces so many memories that the material is very hard to manage.

I have tried to deal with only one aspect of my life, my interest and activity in the Church and yet, even in this restricted area, I have found it impossible to include everything I could have wished.

What I have written makes me appear a very 'one-sided' person, but I assure those who do not know me that I have many other interests which don't lie within the scope of this book, and those who do, that the reason they are not included is not because I do not love them nor because I am not grateful for the influence they have had upon me, but because they do not fit into the limits I set myself which were to record the people and things in the Church which I have found amusing as I look back on them.

It may be a trivial record, but I hope it is illuminated by love and I think I have made myself as ridiculous as anyone at whom I have poked fun.

I
Henfield

———

I HAVE BEEN A PRIEST of the Church of England for over thirty years. This is not a very long time compared with some of the old gentlemen who still live in the country vicarages which they have inhabited for almost twice that period.

I preached for one this autumn in his church, not far from a large industrial town, and in the forty years he has been incumbent he has put electricity in neither the church nor the vicarage. The whole experience reminded me vividly of clerical life as I knew it in my boyhood and I had forgotten how comfortable it was. The dim interior of the church with hissing lamps and guttering candles so different from harsh and hideous strip lighting. The open fires in every room of the vicarage and the sitting long over a boiled fowl and a bottle of claret while discussing church politics in a very party fashion reminded me of an age which has passed.

It was a comfort to feel that these things have not completely vanished for I am sometimes tempted to think that the Church of England in which I grew up has disappeared entirely.

Yet what a variety of changes in thought and attitude, as well as external practice, I have myself experienced since I was led, rather reluctantly, to my first church service in the old parish church of St. Peter in Henfield, Sussex, where my parents lived.

We had, as a family, no clerical connections. My father was a dyer and cleaner and belonged to a Jacobite family which had crossed the border many years before; and eighteenth-century correspondence shows that they were very acrimonious elders of the Crown Court Presbyterian Church in London.

There was an eighteenth-century cleric connected with the family whose name was Ball and a funeral ode exists, the last verse of which reads:

> 'So each of us when death doth call
> In his appointed place
> Shall join the Choir with Mr. Ball
> And sing redeeming Grace.'

When the Stephensons joined the Established Church of England I have no idea, but by the time that I was born the Presbyterian strain had been eliminated, for my father's aunt, who lived at Redhill, was a pillar of the establishment, and his mother, by whom he was most strongly influenced, had been swept into Tractarianism and even 'went to confession to the Bishop of Lewes'—a combination of things which gave me a very high opinion of her, although I had no personal memories, when I first began to appreciate ecclesiastical distinctions.

My mother came from an Irish family called Flinn, who gave their name to the dyeing and cleaning business, and her father was, I believe, a lapsed Roman Catholic, who expressed his anti-clerical feelings by insisting on eating salt pork on Good Friday which he thought would upset the bishops—though how they were expected to know I doubt if he ever considered!

The Flinns' cleaning activities were centred on Brighton and so it was difficult for them not to dye in the true faith, as will be seen, and that is why my memories and experience of the church have always been almost exclusively confined to what is known as the 'high' section of Anglicanism.

The small boy who was being led down the narrow path across the fields to Henfield Church where the bells were issuing an imperative summons had been taught to say his prayers—mostly about lambs and shepherds—and to make the sign of the cross, which he did with such gusto and at such very inappropriate moments that I think his mother rather regretted showing him how.

My father was one of the churchwardens, so I think that I must have been taken along at an earlier age than most children for it was not then usual for parents to bring babes in arms and it would have been thought rather irreverent to carry them to the altar rails, as is now quite common. I was not expected at first to stay for the sermon, but I soon discovered that if I yawned very noisily I was taken home at once. I could not see much of what was going on in the chancel, but I rather enjoyed getting right down in the pew and looking at the legs of those in front, many of whom leaned forward on the edge of the seat and did not kneel, so that I got a good view of their rumps.

The church at Henfield is most attractively situated away from the High Street and its shops which grew up on the main Horsham-Brighton road, and is set well back amongst old cottages—one of which is called 'The Cat House', a name liable to mislead Americans! This title is not at all ancient and comes from the fact that the old thatched building has cats killing canaries cut out of tin, which were used as a decoration and put up to torment poor old Canon Woodard (founder of the schools) who had retired to a house near the church where his cat per-petrated this fatal act and earned him the undying hatred of the owner of the cottage—who not only put up a visible memento of the crime, but blew 'raspberries' through an aperture (which he named a 'Zuluhole') at the poor old Canon as he went to church, finally forcing him to walk right round the village in order to get there without passing the scene of the murder.

The churchyard is full of tidily clipped yews and the church itself is mainly twelfth century with a fine square tower on top of which spins St. Peter's cock as a weather vane. Inside it has been much restored at the wrong period. There was too much money in the South when Victorian ecclesiological enthusiasm was at its height.

I think it is the smell inside which I recall most vividly. That unmistakable Anglican smell compounded of gas, old hymn books, hassocks and surplices all permeated with the fumes of the coke boiler, the heat from which came up through rather frightening gratings in the floor, down one of which I once lost a very precious marble I had taken out to beguile me during the more tedious and incomprehensible phrases of the Litany—always sung on the first Sunday in the month.

The interior of the church had been spoiled by a superfluity of pews made of pitch-pine and stained a particularly disagree-able shade of orange. The organ had been bought secondhand from the Brighton Aquarium, where presumably its function had been to entertain the spectators rather than the fish. The front pipes, from under which the surpliced choir emerged from the

11

vestry, were painted with rather gaudy gothic patterns; but its internals had never recovered from life in the Aquarium and there was apt to be a strange gurgling sound from time to time which was only controlled when the ancient organist stuffed a long stick with an alms bag on the end into its vitals.

The large east window had been filled with glass by Kemp, who had designed most of the smaller windows in the church. It was his very first commission and he was rather ashamed of it. Later in life, when he was famous, he offered to replace it at his own expense, but by this time the parishioners had become rather fond of it and refused to have it changed.

This conservatism seemed to extend to everything that had got into the church in the way of ornament. Although I did not know about such things at that time, I came to realise that the high altar was very lamentable. It was too small, had an ugly brass cross and was surrounded by rather badly carved woodwork of debased gothic design. Yet any suggestion that it should be replaced roused passions to fever pitch.

The carving had been done by local boys under the direction of a former curate called Divie Robertson (I reproduce the name as it remains in my mind for I do not think I ever saw it in writing). He had gone off to South America and been drowned which had effectively canonised his memory so that any plan for altering the chancel he had helped to decorate was treated as near blasphemy.

After the war a vicar, braver than his predecessors, had the whole thing changed and my mother, who was giving the new altar ornaments in memory of my father, was tormented by letters from the 'old guard' telling her how unpopular the whole scheme was and how they were sure she would not wish my father's name to be linked with something which was so disliked in the village. They had a partial victory for the sacred wood-work, in all its horror, was re-erected in the south transept. Now there is some scheme which would leave the high altar orna-ments looking too large and already it is being said how dis-tressed my mother would have been to see them removed.

This hatred of change is a very Anglican attitude and one can understand how maddened lay people were when the first Tractarian vicars abolished the cosy box pews and three-decker pulpits and substituted the pitch-pine pews and encaustic tiles which the later generation guard so jealously.

The Vicar of Henfield when I was a boy was a particularly handsome and distinguished looking man whose churchmanship was what I later learned to call 'middle-stump' Anglicanism. He must have been a little to the high side of centre for during his time the Parham Chantry was rather nicely restored as a chapel and linen vestments came into use. I do not think that these robes are nowadays much in favour, but at that time they were considered to look from the distance of the nave enough like a long surplice to fool the less vigilant protestants.

The local chemist claimed to have been responsible for this innovation. He had come from London and had learned 'what-was-what' at some high church in Vauxhall. He was the first person I ever noticed genuflecting and I thought it must be some disease and was surprised that the highly coloured bottles in the window of his emporium did not supply a remedy.

Later when he discovered that I was sympathetic in matters of churchmanship he would accompany the purchase of some laxative pills with a few Liturgical observations during which he told me with some pride that he had said to the vicar, when he was counting the collection after the early service, that surely he could not go on 'poking about in a surplice at the altar for ever'. This he claimed was what had led to the introduction of linen vestments, and I wondered what I could say to the vicar which would embolden him to take the next step and introduce the real thing.

The path of advancing churchmanship had not, however, been without difficulties. While I was fairly young a mission had been held in the parish for a week. How this came about I do not know, but the vicar must have been feeling particularly bold as he invited as Missioner the vicar of one of the most 'extreme' Anglo-Catholic churches in Brighton.

He was called 'Father' Carey. The mystique of why the names of some clergy in the Church of England are prefixed by the word 'Father' and others are not is never easy to explain, nor where exactly the dividing line comes. A certain section of the laity adopt it with great enthusiasm and some almost put it between words saying, 'Good Father, night Father'. It is, however, easier to explain than the popular use of the term 'Padre' which is the same thing in Spanish, but often used by those who think 'Father' too high church.

Father Carey brought some nuns to help with the mission

and one of them came to lunch with us. I was enormously impressed and gazed across the table at this strange figure as if she were a visitant from another planet, while my mother appeared to behave as though she were. For some reason I cannot now begin to understand, I thought she was a Jew, and told several people that we had a Jew to luncheon and that she had worn a napkin on her head.

Many years later, after I had become a priest, a Sister of the Society of St. Margaret, East Grinstead, gave me greetings from an old Sister who was in the infirmary and who had told her that she had met me as a small boy. It must have been the Jew!

The mission was not appreciated by everybody for Father Carey had used the dreaded word 'Mass' and had suggested that people ought to go to confession. When at a meeting of the Parochial Church Council someone suggested that a vote of thanks should be communicated to the Missioner my father's fellow-churchwarden arose and delivered a fearsome denunciation of popery.

From this time my father was regarded as the champion of the high church faction, and this was visibly demonstrated at the presentation of the alms. My father would always stand at the chancel step facing the altar till the plate was elevated, while the low church warden would scuttle back to his seat the moment he had delivered his bag. This placed the sidesmen in a quandary and some remained with my father while others 'went to earth' at once. It was with great satisfaction that we saw the tide gradually turn until poor Mr. Welch, the protestant champion, was left to give solitary witness to low church principles.

He was, however, strongly supported by an Irish lady called Miss Gubbins, who was very tall and entirely unable to argue without losing her temper, which she did constantly at village meetings of all sorts. On the subject of religion she was, like many of the Irish, particularly violent and would set about the vicar at the church door if she had detected any fresh signs of popery in the service. I have an idea that the vicar would have been prepared to introduce a little more ritualism in a quiet way if he had not been quite so scared of 'the dragon at the door'.

The vicar's wife, on the other hand, was quite capable of dealing with Miss Gubbins—or indeed anyone else in the parish. She was also tall and commanding, usually wearing what appeared to be a baroque dog-collar made of lace and held erect by small whale bones. To a small boy, like myself, she seemed rather severe and forbidding, and certainly had what is known as presence. She provided the perfect foil for her husband whose good nature made him reluctant to say 'no' to anyone or to disagree with anything unless forced to do so. She was rather wealthy, being a member of a famous biscuit making firm, and drove round the parish in a Daimler car with a very smart chauffeur. She appeared to pay for everything like choir treats and bell-ringers' suppers, and enough soup was issued from the vicarage kitchen to float a battleship. When there was a new vicar it was a constant irritation to the parishioners to be asked to subscribe to these things. 'He's always asking for money', they said resentfully.

A tale was told in the village that when the vicar had become engaged someone had said to him : 'I hear you've taken the biscuit!' and he replied : 'Yes, and I've got the tin too.' What gave this story a touch of authenticity was that he was very fond of jokes and puns of this sort, but he never managed to take his sense of humour into the pulpit with him and his sermons were long and boring. It was observed that when he said : 'Just one last thought', it usually went on for longer than the rest of the discourse.

As he got older he became very absent-minded and would read the names of the monarch and royal family from any Prayer Book he happened to take up. As there were some very old ones lying about the church, it provided quite a lesson in English history.

After I became lit-up by Anglo-Catholicism I tried hard to convert him and once gave him a tract which I felt sure could not fail to convince him. A few days later he returned it to me saying : 'I think this might interest you. Someone or other gave it to me, but I've not read it myself. It seems to be more in your line.'

My impression of the 1920s is that almost everyone in the village went to church. This was certainly not so, but to a child it appeared like that. All the people who served one in the shops or whom one encountered in the village during the week in various ways seemed to be in church at Matins on Sunday. The choir was large and made a terrific din while the congregation stood stiffly with Prayer Books, which they had carried to church with them, for in those days the contents were still used

15

and we did not expect to have a small library thrust into our hands by a sidesman the moment we got inside the door.

There was something very impressive about this worshipping community and as I look today at the often pitifully tiny congregations in many village churches I find myself wondering where they have all gone, and I fear the answer is to their graves having failed to convince my generation of the existence of God.

I cannot remember how I was taught the Christian religion for I certainly never went to Sunday School; that was for 'village children' and silly middle-class snobbery kept me out of that category. I do not recall that my parents spoke to me much about spiritual things, except to teach me to say my prayers and insist that I went to church. Once or twice I was taken to a children's service which was held on Sunday afternoons and the vicar once asked if I would like to choose a hymn and I chose 333 because I thought it would look such fun on the board. It proved rather unsuitable in content and I was not asked to choose again.

During the service I enjoyed looking through the Prayer Book I had brought clutched in my little hot hand and which normally was kept at home in a drawer of the hall table. I particularly liked the Latin titles over the psalms which made them seem very mysterious, and of course I was riveted by the Table of Kindred of Affinity with its intriguing information that I was not allowed to marry my grandmother—a perverse possibility which I had never even considered, although I was very given at that time to announcing I was going to marry anyone of any age who took my fancy.

I think that I must have been born with a great love of the mysterious and I invested everything connected with the parish church, the building and all its fittings, with a romanticism which at that time the latter hardly justified. There was a chapel in the High Street which I had always thought to be Methodist until recently I read the board outside and discovered that it describes itself as 'Free Evangelical'. I was once taken inside by my elderly nurse to see a wedding which was taking place in which she had some interest. She had even more interest in funerals and was always claiming to have heard the knell ringing from the church tower and speculating whose death it might be proclaiming. I fancy that this maudlin preoccupation was not unconnected with frequent little visits to the pub, during which

I was left outside and on account of which I was finally removed from her care.

The interior of the chapel left no impression upon me for I was immediately entranced by the sight of Mr. Tobit, the eccentric and wealthy grocer, sitting up very high in front of us all and playing the organ while he swayed too and fro in time with the musical sugar he was dispensing. I was sworn to secrecy about this visit but I did not keep my vow, as I had done solemnly about the trips to the pub, because I could not resist telling my mother how peculiar Mr. Tobit had looked playing the organ. She was very angry indeed, and in these ecumenical days it is hard to realise that with her 'high' Anglican background she really thought dissent was wicked. Certainly the result was that the same irrational feeling was conveyed to me and I never again went inside a dissenting chapel until a few years ago and even now it gives me a vague feeling of guilt.

Besides the church and the chapel there were only two other places of worship in Henfield. One was in a private garden and had a board reading 'Rehoboth, Strict Baptist Chapel', but it appeared to be so strict that I never once saw anyone go in or out of it. The other was a green tin hut which had no board outside but was known in the village as 'Joseph Johnson's Chapel'.

Joseph Johnson was the rather dour Clerk to the Parish Council and had a gloomy little office in a curious building in the High Street called 'The Assembly Rooms', where village functions of all sorts, from badminton to the weekly silent film show, took place. Why he had a chapel of his own I do not know, but I suppose that all these funny little places of worship represented some strong-minded person who had refused to toe the line about something in their own sect. Perhaps he was one degree stricter than Rehoboth!

Once when I was taking a walk with my dog the door of Joseph Johnson's chapel was open and the old spaniel darted in, I following on his heels. There were only four women sitting in a row and before them Joseph Johnson was standing with an open Bible in one hand while the other was raised in some fierce denunciation. As I appeared he stopped and glared and then said in a voice of thunder: 'There is an intruder in our midst'. The women all turned round and I fled.

There was really not much alternative to being C. of E.,

but then the wealthy daughter of a former Vicar of Henfield became a convert to Roman Catholicism and erected a tin hut on her land to serve as an R.C. church. This caused quite a stir in the village and I often heard it implied that the lady had done it under extreme pressure from 'Them', who were presumably the Roman Catholic hierarchy, although I doubt whether those who said these things knew quite whom they meant, and I suspect thought we were the victims of some deeply laid plan which had been hatched in the Vatican.

Once a church was built other Roman Catholics came to live in the village and began to form quite a colony. There was one dear old lady who sold sweets, which I often bought, who told me that her husband had been a Carthusian lay brother. 'He loved it', she said piously, 'until he met me'.

To shepherd this flock came an enchanting Belgian priest who had come over to England as a refugee during the first war to look after his exiled compatriots and had decided to stay on in this country and take in foreign boys who wanted to learn English, which he did to the delight and deflowering of a number of the local girls.

Fr. Van, as he was known, was simple, friendly and patently holy so that all the village came to love him and he did more than anything to break down the prejudice that there was against R.Cs. They were treated—and indeed behaved—very much as a race apart.

When the son of the lady who had built their church started a pig farm in the middle of the village, Miss Gubbins organised a protest saying: 'I can forgive him being a Roman Catholic and I can forgive him keeping pigs, but I can't forgive both.' The protest was not very successful as the Health Official who was sent to inspect the piggery gave it high commendation and said that he wished more people would keep them.

What first prompted me to go inside the R.C. church I do not know, but I was at once enraptured by the smell of incense and the small winking lamps. I began buying tracts and prayer books from the back of the church. They were mostly of Irish origin and I soon discovered that they needed to be used with care, for in the middle of reciting an effusion in honour of the Sacred Heart I turned the page and discovered in time that I was about to take a vow of abstinence from alcoholic liquor for the rest of my life.

Oddly enough it never occurred to me for a moment that I might become a Roman Catholic for I did not at all like the sound of 'Them' who had kindled the embers of the fires of Smithfield which every Englishman has smouldering in his unconscious. Yet my immediate reaction was, 'This is what the Church of England ought to be like.' So strong and emphatic was this feeling that, even if the Oxford Movement had not taken place, I really think I might have had the idea.

Because of this new interest in the Roman Catholic church I ventured to visit Cowfold Monastery which was not far away, but which had always seemed to be an unknown land. Amongst my earliest memories was waking in the night and hearing the bell ringing from the monastery when the wind was in the right direction. Once when hiding in a wood not far from home I had heard voices and suddenly into the clearing—which I could see from my lair—came a party of the strangest looking men I had ever encountered. They were all dressed in white and had completely shaven heads with flowing beards. They seemed to be talking in a foreign language as, oblivious of my presence they crossed the glade and moved out of sight. I reported this extraordinary experience at home and was told that it was some of the monks from Cowfold on their weekly walk.

Parkminster, Cowfold, was founded by Carthusians when the religious orders were suppressed in France in the last century. They are an order of collective hermits, each monk living in an isolated house around a great cloister and joining together only in church and eating together only on Sundays and Feast Days. They keep silence except for their weekly walk, which I had seen them taking, but I have been told that they do not find much to talk about as they never see a newspaper or hear the radio.

After the Great War one of the monks, a German, simply refused to believe that Germany had been defeated, but there was no way of proving it to him. In 1940, during the Battle of Britain, a German plane was shot down in their grounds and the monk, who was still alive, said smugly: 'What did I tell you, the Fatherland still fights on!'

It was with great excitement that I pulled the chain beside the monastery door and heard a bell sound within. After a few moments the bolts were pulled back and a very old monk, bent with age, looked down upon my diminutive person with a kindly

19

eye. I later discovered that he had been the porter for many years and was a lay-brother called George.

He showed me into a small room when I said that I wanted to see the monastery and told me that I must wait till the Guest Master came around. He then went back to his Porter's Lodge leaving me alone. I sat on the edge of a chair feeling rather nervous for I had heard the bolts of the main door grind back into place. I felt that I might indeed have put myself into the hands of 'Them' and I had told no one where I was going.

There was the sound of steps approaching along the cloister and I was beginning to wish I had never entered the trap when the door opened and a monk with a bright red beard came in, asked my age and said : 'Ah! so you want to be a monk do you?'

It was Brother Francis, the Guest Master, and it was a joke; but I was horrified. However he soon put me at my ease for he was one of the merriest men I have ever met, always making jokes and roaring with laughter.

We soon became great friends and I think my parents were a little worried as, when asked where I had been I would as like as not reply airily : 'Oh, just up to the monastery.'

Brother Francis was a Scot, but he had been for so many years shut up with an almost entirely French community that he spoke English with a Scottish-French accent which sounded most peculiar. He was much amused by my youthful enthusiasm and endless questions and he was quite uninhibited in asking why I did not belong to the 'True Church'. He also told me that he was going to perform all sorts of penances for my conversion. It used to make me feel rather a cad when he would ask : 'Well, are you converted yet?' and I was forced to answer 'No', but his eyes were twinkling with laughter.

More extraordinary was my contact with the Procurator, who is like a bursar and the only Father to have contact with the outside world. He had occasion to write to me more than once on a very old typewriter which had certain peculiarities and so enabled me to know the source of certain anonymous and very crude proselytising tracts which came through the mail after I was ordained. It seemed to me so odd that anyone living an enclosed and contemplative life could bother about the party line. On the other hand I suppose that if you really believe that outside the Roman Communion there can be no salvation you must make every effort to rescue the perishing.

Unless of course you can be like the woman who once said to me: 'I'm not at all bigoted, I believe that when Protestants die they become Roman Catholics!'

As I came to the monastery so often when there were no other visitors about, Brother Francis would take me to parts which were not usually on view. Once he hid me in the great cloister when the bell began to ring for Vespers so that I could see the Fathers come quietly out of their little houses and pass like silent ghosts down the long vaulted way which led to the church. Often he would take me into one of the little houses which was not occupied and say: 'This we have reserved for you when you join us.'

I was particularly fascinated by the paintings in the Chapter House which depicted, with horrible realism, the suffering of the Carthusian martyrs at the Reformation. Brother Francis would describe the act of disembowelling with apparent relish.

It has since seemed odd to me that these mild and gentle souls should have surrounded themselves with such macabre and blood-thirsty pictures, but I think the desire for martyrdom still plays a considerable part in their spirituality and the thought of death is a regular meditation.

Once when I arrived the door was not opened by Brother George, the old porter, and Brother Francis told me he had died and led me to the lay-brothers' chapel where he was lying surrounded by candles as if he were asleep or made of wax. It was the first time I had ever seen a dead person but Brother Francis told me that they did not use coffins and that he would be laid in the earth just as he was, in his habit with his hood pulled over his head.

I suppose it was unusual to subject a young boy to this experience, but they seemed to regard death as so natural that I was not nearly as upset as my mother when I described the whole thing to her on my return home.

Certainly these contacts with monasticism—and as I now realise in one of its most dramatic forms—had an enormous influence on the romantic streak in me. I loved to see the monks moving silently about the cloisters and bowing profoundly whenever they passed the end of the church where the Blessed Sacrament was reserved. As the Fathers came into chapel they each took a turn at tolling the bell before the high altar till all had assembled. If someone did not appear it was presumed that

21

he was dead or seriously ill and his house was at once entered. Otherwise his enclosure was inviolate.

Brother Francis did not disguise from me that it was a very austere life and he showed me the little scourge with which they did corporal penance in their cells. Once when I persuaded him to leave me alone and locked in one of the little houses I gave myself a few swipes with the discipline, but it made me giggle and I have never since been able to take that form of asceticism very seriously.

He told me that I had already remained in a cell longer than some aspirants to the order, for the shortest stay had been a priest who was locked into his house and twenty minutes later had come shooting through the kitchens, out of the back door, and was never seen again.

At one time I took to cycling up to the monastery almost every day during my school holidays and attending Vespers, sitting alone in the gallery high above the monastic choir and listening to the slow, pure plainchant which had something almost disembodied about it. It did not make me feel that I wanted to join the Roman Church, but it fired my imagination with the idea of founding a monastery within the Church of England. It was some years before I discovered that it had already been done.

2

Brighton

A VERY MOMENTOUS EVENT in my religious life was the day when I decided on an impulse to investigate the extraordinary building which I had often seen from the train as I entered Brighton railway station. It towered above the houses like two tall narrow brick buildings which had got stuck on top of each other. I had often noticed it, but one day having a little time to spare before returning to Henfield (for I had now graduated to being allowed to travel by myself) I decided I would go and find out what it was.

Thus I first pushed open the door of the church of St. Bartholomew and was quite overcome by its size and magnificence. There was a whole altar made of silver, like something off my mother's dressing table, and the high altar was so vast that I imagined elephants might come in from either side and look like poodles. Along the sides were great confessional boxes which seemed as if the Royal Pavilion had had puppies, and the Stations of the Cross were half life-size.

From my experience of Cowfold Monastery and the Roman Catholic church at Henfield I immediately recognised the religion, but largely for something to say asked the woman, who was reading a book at the back and looked up as if expecting conversation, whether this was a Roman Catholic church?

To my surprise she looked rather cross and said : 'No, it is not, it's Church of England', as if she could not think what had put such an idea into my head and immediately lowered her eyes again to her book.

I felt rather squashed, but also very exultant because it seemed like a dream come true. For some time I had wished that the C. of E. could be more like the R.C. church as I had come to know it, and here it looked identical. In a moment I was completely won over without any intellectual difficulties, and knowing nothing whatever about it I thought to myself: 'This is the religion I'm going to have and I shall come here to church.' It was certainly a 'conversion experience' at the age of ten, but I doubt whether Evangelicals would consider it very valid.

Looking back it is a surprise to me that I was left to discover St. Bart's on my own for when I got home and told my mother of the wonderful church I had found she not only revealed that she knew all about it but that she had been there herself when she was a girl. She also said that the best time to go was at the great festivals when they had a full orchestra in the gallery at the back.

Far from raising any opposition to my going there she agreed to take me herself and said that she had rather missed it over the years since she left Brighton. Furthermore I discovered that my grandmother had known Fr. Wagner, who had built St. Bart's and several other Brighton churches. When I talked to her about it she told me that she remembered that when it was being built there were rumours that the bays one could see in the foundations were cells into which nuns were to be walled. In my romantic excitement about medieval monasticism I was rather sorry it had been a mistake.

My grandmother's position in all this is something of a mystery to me as I never knew her to darken the door of a church. In fact I never really knew her to do anything very much as at an early age she had decided that she was an invalid and hardly ever left the house, even having a night nurse for as long as I can remember. In this way she kept herself alive to the age of ninety-six. She must at one time have come under the sway of Fr. Wagner, as she had my mother brought up in that sort of religion although other members of her family, of which my mother was the youngest, appeared to have missed it.

When she realised that I had become interested she would sometimes tell me disjointed reminiscences such as that once when she had been to St. Paul's Church, West Street, a hostile crowd had thrown mud at them as they came out from the service. She did not seem to remember why this demonstration had taken place, but I think it must have been at the time when a murderess at her trial had revealed that she had been to confession to Fr. Wagner some weeks before giving herself up to the police, and protestant propaganda represented St. Paul's as a den of iniquity.

I cannot remember if it was then she told me that attending St. Paul's was known as 'going to the Sunday opera', but I wish that I had asked her more about this part of her life for she must have given it all up as I never remember a priest calling upon her. Perhaps it was only a passing phase for some of the things she told me were very muddled and she did not seem to understand what the fuss had been about. 'They used to say "Old Wagner wants to put the clock back" ', she once told me and added meditatively: 'I suppose he must have had something to do with the introduction of summer time.'

Arthur Wagner was, in fact, the apostle of Anglo-Catholicism in Brighton. With my discovery of St. Bart's I began to learn about the Movement in the Church of England which had brought it into being. Put briefly and crudely the history as I picked it up was as follows:

The Middle Ages were the high point of Christianity in England. The Reformation was a complete disaster and deprived the ordinary Englishman of the full practice of the Catholic religion which was his by right. A small group had remained in communion with the Pope and were called "Recusants"; they were brave, but wrong-minded. For two hundred years the Church of England got deader and deader and the sacraments fell into disuse. Then a gallant group of men in Oxford decided to change all this and they were subjected to terrible persecution until one of them called John Henry Newman "went over" to Rome taking a lot of other people with him. They were very wrong, but the blame lay with those who persecuted them.

A very brave old man called Dr. Pusey endured everything and gathered round him a lot of daring young priests who began to have the right sort of services and to convert people to believe the right things. There were others called Protestants who did their best to stop them and even got the law changed so that they could send right-minded priests to jail, which they proceeded to do. Almost all the bishops were Protestants and not to be trusted. However the fight was still going on and Anglo-Catholics were right and everyone else was wrong.

This of course is an over-simplification, but it is more or less what I was taught at a very impressionable age and although it is almost entirely incorrect and I learned to see this with my mind I continued to react emotionally as if it were truth itself, and probably still do when taken unawares.

Just as I had begun to learn doctrine from Roman Catholic tracts so I picked up Church history from Anglo-Catholic tracts and a lot of very curious ideas I got from both, but this went on over a course of several years and by then I regarded myself as a fully paid-up party member.

The first High Mass I attended at St. Bart's was a great event in my life. It was Easter Day and there were crowds of people pouring into the enormous church which, big as it was, was already becoming short of seats. Fortunately I was at the end of a row so that I could step out into the aisle and see what was happening. The only snag was that my mother rather disapproved of this sort of behaviour in church and would keep pulling me back.

I discovered that this same puritanism made her object to sitting down during the singing of the Creed and Gloria, which took a very long time as they were always sung to elaborate settings. In this she was joined by a small band of spartans who looked very conspicuous dotted over the large seated congregation. I was much mortified when a little friend said to me: 'I notice your mother was one of those old trees.'

We did not have to wait long before things started to happen, for a door opened halfway down the nave and a rotund man wearing a cassock and cotta entered proceeded by a small boy carrying a pile of music. He walked solemnly down the aisle bowing graciously on either side to those with whom he was acquainted. I discovered that this was Mr. Madle the organist who was responsible for the musical tradition of St. Bart's. When Cyril Tomkinson became the vicar he was apt to say to people: 'I help a little at Mr. Madle's church.'

Mr. Madle used to set the Kyries to famous operatic airs and put on the Music List 'Gluck-Madle' or 'Mozart-Madle'; but all these refinements I was to learn later.

Once he reached the gallery at the back of the church the organ swirled into life and in the background I could hear stringed instruments tuning-up, a sound which never ceased to excite me however often I heard it in church, for it was

26

indeed a promise of delights to come and I can understand what the disaffected meant when they spoke of 'the Sunday opera'. At the same time a server appeared on the ledge behind the altar walking between the candlesticks as he lit them and giving some idea of the vast scale of the church and its fittings.

Arthur Wagner must have been a man of extraordinary imagination for he brought into being these basilica-like churches and when the Brighton Corporation, horrified by the height of St. Bart's, refused permission for another building of the same proportions, he excavated for the Church of the Resurrection so that one entered at the head of a mighty flight of steps. It did not withstand the damp very well and by the time I knew it it had already been turned into a refrigerated meat store. No wonder his father, the Vicar of Brighton, seeing his son pouring away the family fortune in these extraordinary buildings preached from the text: 'Lord have mercy on my son, for he is a lunatic.' It was a time when texts were much used in this way and it is recounted that once when after some trouble Fr. Wagner sacked both his curates the sermon was preached on the text: 'Stay ye here with the ass, while I and the lad go yonder.'

I am sorry I never knew him for I owe him a lot for the monuments he left behind, which to a great extent formed my opinion of what the Church of England ought to look like. He lived to a ripe old age having built churches with careless abandon and founded a Sisterhood, which in those days was a *sine qua non* for any Anglo-Catholic priest worth his salt. He became rather senile and it is nice to think that when the statue of Queen Victoria was erected to commemorate her Diamond Jubilee he died happy in the thought that his life's work had been crowned and the Brighton Corporation, who had prevented some of his more ambitious schemes, had erected an image of Our Blessed Lady.

All these things I learned much later when I had grown quite accustomed to High Mass at St. Bart's, but it never again gave me quite the thrill of that first experience. The large choir lined up in front of the high altar with old men carrying almost a dozen banners (I was told by some later vicar that these old men never appeared at any other time, but by some tribal instinct seemed to know when there was to be a procession). In the distance a bell tinkled which brought us all to our feet and by stepping out into the aisle I could see the tops of candles being carried in front of the choir and the little black hats of the sacred ministers as they took their places before the altar.

Although I did not know then that the little round hats with pom-poms were called 'birettas', I immediately guessed that they were very special for I had never before seen a clergyman wearing one and it was not long before I regarded them as the very hall-mark of sound churchmanship.

There was a dramatic silence only broken by the clank of the censer chains as incense was put on and a column of blue smoke began to rise. Then a rather cracked voice intoned, 'Let us proceed in peace', but peace was not to be the order of the day, for the tympani began to roll and then with a crash of full organ and orchestra the procession set off singing 'Hail thee festival day' in a tumult of sound. I was spellbound by all this and delighted when they came past me so that I could get a proper look at them. There was a smug little boy even younger than I was who was carrying the incense boat and I envied him very much and determined that I would get his job if I could, a resolution which remained unfulfilled owing to my mother's strange repugnance to let me do anything to call attention to myself. When other small boys were all getting up to recite their party piece and I was bursting to do mine my mother would refuse on my behalf. It is a modern axiom that parents are always wrong and when many years later a doctor was investigating a persistent migraine from which I suffered, he gave as his opinion that this early suppression was its cause.

My attention was not long held by the boat boy for I was riveted by the thurifer and the censer. Every now and then he would swing it in a complete cartwheel which I thought wildly exciting and great clouds of smoke issued forth. To my great delight as he passed us the whole thing burst into flames as a result of his over-vigorous swinging. I had no idea that this was unintentional and was deeply disappointed when it did not happen during the next procession I saw.

At the end were the priests in their richly embroidered vestments and looking rather bored, which was the Anglo-Catholic liturgical face par excellence. But perhaps they were bored, for Fr. Cyril Tomkinson once said to me : 'I know, my dear, that one ought to have elevated thoughts during these long functions, but I cannot keep my mind off what I'm going to have for luncheon.'

28

And so they returned to the high altar and for the first time the great drama of the Mass was unfolded before me. Looking back over the years I can see that I was right to be deeply impressed, for High Mass at St. Bartholomew's, Brighton, was indeed a very solemn spectacle and performed with great reverence. There was not much congregational participation, but we all went down like a field of corn before the wind at the 'Incarnatus' in the Creed. At the consecration there was a thrilling silence only broken by the tinkling of the bell when the Host was elevated. This silence was the more impressive after the ear-splitting volumes of sound during the singing of the Sanctus.

Of course in those days the late Mass was strictly non-communicating and there would have been great consternation if any members of the congregation had presented themselves for Holy Communion. Yet there was a wonderful feeling of holiness and worship which, young as I was, conveyed itself to me. Never from that moment was there any difficulty about getting me to go to church and I loved every moment of it.

It was strange to have begun with a church like Bart's, Brighton, for I found later that other churches were a slight disappointment in comparison. I heard tales of the wonderful church of All Saints, Margaret Street, of the great St. Albans, Holborn, and the exotic St. Mary's, Graham Street, and I thought they must be even bigger and finer; but when at last I saw them they appeared rather pokey and mean.

Although I did not know it, I had stumbled upon Anglo-Catholicism at the height of its power as a movement. The mighty Congresses of the 1920s were going on, the great 'centres' were thronged with congregations many of whom came long distances, as we did, and really belonged to other parishes. Persecution on any large scale had more or less ceased and there were even bishops who talked about 'Mass' and wore eucharistic vestments.

Yet for all its triumphalism it held within it the seeds of its own dissolution which the disorganisation of the last war simply accelerated. It had become congregationalist and cut off from the main stream of the Church of England and rejoiced to have it so. It had thrown in its lot devotionally with the baroque Catholicism of the continent just when that movement was about to be discredited in the church of its origin, and looking at it now one realises that it had about as much chance of appealing to the average Anglican as the Folies Bergères to the Mothers' Union.

I remember a meeting of Anglo-Catholics in the 1930s when a suffragan bishop said : 'The ball is at our feet if we will all play the same game.' It was a fond hope for Anglo-Catholic clergy all had their own tiny Vatican of infallible 'do's and don'ts' which they would maintain in spite of any other authority.

Not long ago a friend speaking of an elderly priest who had died said : 'He epitomised everything which is wrong with the Catholic Movement in the C. of E.' He was a snob, constantly saying : "Things aren't what they were. There used to be Princess Marie Louise, Lord Halifax" etc., etc., counting out distinguished names like beads on a rosary. He was a gossip, always passing on malicious little bits of information about fellow clergy and denigrating any who seemed successful. He was quarrelsome with his parishioners, even sending solicitor's letters to several before he arrived in a parish. They retaliated in good measure and he was a famous emptier of churches. In one parish they even hired a bus to take them to the next village. Of all these things he was completely unconscious of any fault on his side and would say peevishly in his old age : 'These young priests today have no love of souls.'

Of course at the time of which I am writing I was not even dimly aware of any of these things. As we lived outside Brighton it was a long time before I knew any priests, except very superficially, and to me they all seemed perfect and the sort of Anglo-Catholicism at St. Bart's something which people had only to be shown to be as instantly converted as I had been.

It is a measure of my innocence that it never occurred to me that the religion of the Middle Ages which seemed to me so romantic would have had only a superficial resemblance to what I had discovered at Bart's. It has been argued that had the Reformation never happened the Church in England would have undergone the same influences which shaped Catholicism on the continent, but it was long time before it ever dawned on me that such an argument was needed. I thought that the deposit of all truth lay within the towering walls of St. Bartholomew's; well might Anglo-Catholicism be called 'the London, Brighton and South Coast religion'.

But a horrid shock awaited me when I was sent as a boarder to a preparatory school in Brighton. What enquiries, apart from asking about the fees, my parents had made before consigning their son to this academy I do not know, but it seemed strange to me that devout churchpeople, as they undoubtedly were, should have made no enquiry about the religion. We were, I discovered, taken on Sundays to attend the lowest church in Brighton.

There were other aspects of the school which were far from satisfactory and most of the masters had more past than future —but these were things which only dawned on me later in life. I reacted against the religion at once; my mother was always telling me it could not be as bad as I reported, but it was. We had prayers every morning at breakfast after we had been dosed with codliver oil and malt. An enormous Bible was brought to the table and one of the masters, who usually showed signs of the previous night's debauch, simply opened it at random and read a long and incomprehensible chapter from one of the minor prophets. We then all knelt with our heads on our chairs while a few prayers off a card were read perfunctorily.

On Sunday evenings we had a solid hour of hymn-singing and were stirred up to put pennies in a box for something called 'The Zenana Mission'. It was many years before I discovered that there was not a diocese of Zenana for I secretly hoped it might be high and have a bishop such as those from Central Africa I had seen at St. Bart's wearing, wonder of wonders, purple birettas. It did in fact support bible-women who went and did to ladies in harems what was done to us after breakfast.

On Sunday mornings we were cleaned and scrubbed, dressed in Eton collars and marched in a crocodile to a church called St. Margaret's which lay hidden behind the Metropole, an hotel where it was rumoured that a bell was rung to enable week-end guests to get gack to their own rooms before morning tea was served, but I am glad to say this rumour was not circulated in our age group.

St. Margaret's has now been pulled down, but I was never able to get inside later in life (it was always kept locked) so I was unable to check on my early impressions. I should now probably admire it greatly, but then I thought it horrible.

It had two tiers of galleries and we sat in what seemed to

31

correspond to the dress circle at the Theatre Royal, to which I was often taken as a treat; but hard pews replaced the red plush tip-up seats. The pulpit was very tall with a winding staircase and on a level with the top circle. The only enjoyment I can every remember having there was when a visiting clergyman fell down the steps gaining speed as he descended the spiral. The altar was the size of a writing desk and covered with red velvet but I never saw it used except as the resting place of an enormous alms dish. There was no cross or candles and the choir mostly consisted of ladies dressed as if they were going to play Portia in *The Merchant of Venice*. Such female intrusions into the sanctuary were then confined to very 'low' churches and no one would have dreamed we should live to see them in the 'cathedral' of Anglo-Catholicism, All Saints, Margaret Street, where the elaborate music was sung by well-beaten and immaculately collared little boys. A nostalgic picture recently published on the dissolution of the Choir School showed them being taught by a priest who had a cane and a biretta on his desk.

St. Margaret's was rather a pretty building from outside, with a dome and a classical portico in the front, but we were always hustled through a back door and up into our gallery.

The vicar liked to arrive wearing a top hat and a frock coat, but his smiles were all for the elderly ladies bearing down on the church and he did not seem to notice us. I never remember his speaking to us at all. No doubt I am doing him an injustice and I expect he was out under the portico being very gracious after the service, but we left by the back door. Of course I compared him unfavourably with the priests at St. Bart's, who by the time the Angelus had rung and we began to leave the church, the orchestra playing the Triumphal March from *Aida*, had taken off their vestments and were outside, with their birettas flat-a-back on their heads, laughing and joking with everyone.

I was the more frustrated because there was almost opposite the school an Anglo-Catholic church into which I would dart for a few moments when we got back from St. Margaret's, not only for the sake of piety, but because we were unsupervised in the period before lunch for the only time in the week and it was utilised by the older boys for an orgy of sadism which worship at St. Margaret's seemed to have sharpened.

Sometimes there was a procession from this church down the

street—probably for the Rogation—and we watched from the dormitory windows. Most of the boys were very mystified, but I was able to be smugly knowledgeable and to say with pride that they did not make as much smoke as they did at my church.

I looked forward to the holidays when I was able to persuade my mother to take me to St. Bart's while my father went to Matins alone or with my sister. She was older than I and had much earlier expressed her distaste for taking part in public worship by throwing her Prayer Book across the hall and returning to bed of her own volition. This scene was probably provoked by something I had said for as I grew older I discovered it was fairly easy to send her off the 'deep-end'; but she soon found that religion was a good area in which to get her own back and she would call me a 'hypocritical little psalm-smiter' —whatever that may mean; but it made me mad at the time and has remained in my memory.

We fought many verbal battles in some odd places, but none I think more curious than when rock climbing in Cornwall we began to quarrel while negotiating a very difficult face and clung to the cliff high above the sea hurling abuse at each other.

Cornwall played a large part in our young lives for holidays were spent at Looe and there were outings and expeditions all over that haunted peninsula. Once we went down to St. Michael's Mount and visited the little church of St. Hilary not far away, which had become well known for its Nativity Play. This had caused a sensation in the early days of broadcasting and had also brought it to the unwelcome attention of protestants, for its vicar, Fr. Bernard Walke, had transformed a dull church in a remote village into a living expression of the Catholic faith. The church was alive with colour as many local artists had helped with its decoration, and the far west has always been a very arty corner of England. Indeed Bernard Walke's wife was an artist. If I knew that he had a wife it did not surprise me for at that time certain nuances of Anglo-Catholicism were still hidden from me. Nor did I realise that the service taking place that Sunday afternoon was benediction, for Bart's, Brighton, was not as high as that, but the memory has remained of the voices of the Cornish women singing, the haze of incense and the many candles. It has left a vivid impression upon me, but I did not visit the place again for many years and in the meantime it had been a battleground on which protestant societies had fought legal and more shameful battles to impose their point of view on the unwilling parishioners. Bernard Walke was a convinced pacifist and would not allow his people to oppose violence; so like their forefathers at the time of the Reformation, they saw many of the things they loved and considered holy destroyed before their eyes.

When I saw the church again the high altar had been torn out and replaced by a table. Many of the decorations and shrines were still there, but they were neglected and unloved. What shocked me most was the feeling of evil which hung over the whole place and if I did not know from others what it had once been I should have thought my childhood memory was a fabrication.

I met Bernard Walke once in a pub at Mevagissey, where he had retired from the fray, and he looked like an aged and kindly Bohemian in corduroy trousers with a workman's red handkerchief round his neck. He was not very anxious to talk of the troubles at St. Hilary's but he did say with pain in his eyes that he minded about the souls which had been in his care more than the wrecking of the church, but that those who had been devoted were walking to Mass at St. Alwyn's, Hayle, where the faith still continued unhindered.

I have never had much sympathy with ideas of legality applied to the worship of God. One heard a horrid echo of the cry: 'We have a law and by that law he ought to die!' St. Hilary's stands as a sad memorial of the desert which can be made by intolerance and prejudice.

When I started going regularly to St. Bart's with my mother I became conscious of the freemasonry which being Anglo-Catholic provided. It was not only the chemist who recognised a fellow member of the clan for there were various high church ladies who lived in the village and sometimes one or other of them would join us in our excursions to Brighton where we could enjoy a more exalted churchmanship.

We could always be distinguished in the village church because we genuflected at the 'Incarnatus' and to the Blessed Sacrament. There was a great flutter when some newcomer 'went down' because we knew at once there was a new member of the clan.

I was very shocked when I discovered that a great friend of my parents who never came to church had, when he lived in

Brighton, been a keen member of the congregation of St. Bart's. When I taxed him with this he said that if Henfield Church was like Bart's he would go, but as it was not he preferred to stay away.

This was the first time I had come across the peculiarly Anglican attitude of attaching oneself to a particular church or priest and just giving up the worship of God when they are no longer available. A weakness of the Catholic Movement has been that lay-people have tended to adopt Fr. So-and-So's religion, together with his particular foibles, instead of being converted to the Catholic religion. For such people their faith is like the house built upon sand.

This was certainly not how I understood things and I was determined to do all I could to make Henfield Church as much like St. Bart's as possible. I persuaded the vicar to let me serve although there was not much to do; and I was always lending him books and tracts which I felt sure would 'bring him on'. He, dear, kind man, was wonderfully tolerant and, I can see now, somewhat amused. He allowed me to ring a bell in the tower at the consecration and even put a little poem I wrote about it in the parish magazine. He was less complaisant when I burned some incense in the church before the service began to make it smell right.

In all this I was encouraged by the high church ladies who would listen with amusement and interest to my plans for 'spiking' up the church. There was one who was tremendously high and her great uncanonised saint was Mother Sarah of Horbury and Laleham, sometimes known in Anglo-Catholic circles as 'the Divine Sarah'. I later came to know Mother Sarah well and indeed became fond of her, but I could never quite equate the determined and rather tyrannical Mother Superior of fact with the ethereal mystic of whom I had first heard from her devoted admirer.

My friend's devotion was extended to all monks and nuns whom she thought perfect in every way and when I went to see her, as I often did, she would give me a large glass of Buckfast Tonic wine murmuring : 'Made by the monks, you know', as if this made it any more suitable for a young boy. In fact I found it very intoxicating and often went home 'sloshed'.

What my father thought about all these things I do not know for he never talked much about religion although he took his

35

duties as churchwarden very seriously and a lot of his spare time was spent in doing things for others which made him very much loved in the village. After his death I discovered several acts of charity in which he had been engaged and about which his family knew nothing.

It was his custom to go to Holy Communion on the first Sunday in the month, but when a new vicar started a parish communion which was rather unpopular in the village and known for a long time simply as 'the vicar's service', my father felt it his duty to back him up and became a weekly communicant.

This new regime ought to have pleased me very much and was indeed the beginning of a transformation of Henfield as a parish, so that now the Mass has completely replaced Matins and the sacrament is reserved. However with the perversity of youth, for I had by this time left school, I objected to the fact that the new vicar would only give communion into the hands. He was a fanatic about the rubrics of the Book of Common Prayer and when one morning I dragged myself up to go to communion having been at a party till the small hours and fasted rigidly since midnight, he concluded the Mass after the Prayer for the Church Militant because I was the only person present and the Prayer Book said that there should be at least three. It was stupid of me to be upset, but the result was that I went less and less to Henfield Church and more and more to Brighton and to a Convent not far away.

Sometimes my father came to Bart's with my mother and me, but he never made any comment on the service although I did hear him once say that he did not think High Mass was 'quite the done thing'. However he never showed any signs of disapproval and when my sister became engaged to a Roman Catholic and we were having a religious argument, with my mother taking my side as she usually did, my sister suddenly appealed to him although he was taking no part and quietly reading a newspaper. She said: 'You agree with me, Daddy, don't you?' My father, who was a mild man, put down his paper and said with surprising vehemence: 'No, I do not.' My sister rose to her feet with dignity and said: 'It becomes increasingly clear to me that I am the only decent Protestant in a family of bloody Roman Catholics'; and she left the room slamming the door behind her.

3
Cranleigh

IN 1928 I WAS SENT to school at Cranleigh in Surrey which is situated in charming country below the North Downs. Two of my closest friends at the preparatory school came on to Cranleigh at the same time and we were all in the same house.

Neither of these friends shared my religious interests which shows that, although I have presented myself as something of a midget religious maniac, I did in fact have other more usual preoccupations for a boy of my age. One of these friends is now a well-known script-writer for films and television and a master of risqué innuendo who is liable, when my name is mentioned, to say that he still uses the jokes I told him at school! The other is a distinguished ambassador who in those days would get a rise out of me by arguing from a Roman Catholic point of view, although the sentiments he then expressed would now come oddly from the fine establishment figure he is today.

We saw a lot of each other in the holidays, but religion played very little part in our friendship and looking back I am surprised that I never made any Anglo-Catholic friends of my own age.

Cranleigh was a very 'church' school and most of its headmasters had been clerics. Their portraits looked down upon us in the Dining Hall as we ate food, the like of which I did not experience again till a few years ago I was being flown across Canada by an airline which fear of a libel action prevents me from naming. The bewhiskered first headmaster who glared down upon us grimly was named, rather inappropriately, Dr. Merriman.

The original buildings of the school were 'Gothic Revival Convent Style' in decorated brick and the chapel was a noble feature. They belonged to the period of high romance at the end of the last century when it was thought suitable to put boys in a monastic setting and make them so uncomfortable that anything which happened to them later in life would seem comparatively nice. This has been the strength of the public school system which has not yet been completely humanised.

If I had wished for a background to my monastic fantasies, which at that time under the influence of Cowfold Monastery were raging within me, a better one could not have been devised. But had a congress of Carthusian abbots materialised at the moment when my parents drove away and left me it would have brought me little comfort. Even today I can recreate the horrible feeling of desolation as I saw my little island of security disappearing on four wheels and leaving me entirely unprotected.

I had my hand in my trouser pocket, which I soon discovered was enough to get me beaten, but at that moment I was fingering a rosary which I had been given at the monastery. Although I had not yet learned how to perform the devotion, the very feel of it brought me enormous comfort. At night I would go to sleep clutching it in my hand and it gave me a secret feeling of security. During the war when I was in danger I liked to feel my rosary in my pocket and I suppose that it was a recreation of this earlier experience.

I loved the chapel from the first moment I saw the inside, for it reminded me of Cowfold Monastery with the pews facing each other and the headmaster sitting in a raised stall at the west end gazing down on his monks like the Prior.

We were not, however, taught monastic 'custody of the eyes' and I could not think why an older boy in another house kept winking at me for I had yet to learn about many aspects of school life.

At the east end the altar was impressive: elevated on a lot of steps and backed by an elaborate stone reredos depicting the Ascension in which the figure of Our Lord looked strangely like the Bishop of Guildford, who had a beard. When a new and rather uninhibited headmaster came he said that he was glad he could see no representation of the suffragan bishop, whom he much disliked.

There was a red sanctuary lamp hanging in front of the altar, which reminded me of St. Bart's and the frontals were elaborate and heavy with embroidery. The white one had as its central motif the Holy Spirit represented as a dove with a halo which appeared to have a hooked beak. Many years later when a Norfolk squire told me that he could not think why his new vicar kept calling the Holy Ghost a 'parakeet', my mind went back to that frontal which might have given visible proof to his suspicions of doctrinal extravagance.

Various alterations were made in the chapel during my time at school mainly as a result of installing a new organ in the ambulatory behind the altar. This involved the moving of the old instrument with its gurgling water pump and dark recesses where many unsalutary friendships were consummated, for it did not take me long to discover what the winking had been about. Perhaps this was why at the same time as the old organ was removed a rather frightening text reading: 'Be sure your sin will find you out' also disappeared from above the door by which we left the chapel.

In recent times the altar has been whisked out of the sanctuary and deposited on what I believe is called a podium at the other end of the chapel. One has become accustomed to the peripatetic nature of altars in these days, but it was difficult to see what advantage it had and now the forces of reaction have replaced the original altar so that one is reminded of the rude seaside postcard which depicts a comic clergyman saying: 'We have two fonts in our church so that we can baptise babies at both ends.'

The school when I joined had attained a moderately high church convention in its worship which would have delighted the hearts of the Tractarians. The choir robed on Sundays and on Saturday evenings, when we celebrated the 'First Vespers' with some pomp.

From the first moment that I saw the demure line of surplice-clad trebles glide into the chapel I determined to join them and succeeded in disguising my tone deafness when we were tested so that I was soon imploring the deity for the wings of a dove in honied tones which drew admiring glances from older boys who were starting on that romantic quest which was likely to lead to an invitation behind the organ.

1928 was the great year of the Prayer Book controversy but I do not remember it causing me any concern although I was conscious that it was going on. Tempers amongst churchmen were running high and the Bishop of Exeter is recorded as saying: 'It is an extremely dishonest book put together by honest men.' Hensley-Henson, the waspish Bishop of Durham, delighted Anglo-Catholics by writing 'The Evangelical Party are an army of illiterates led by octogenarians'; but their satisfaction was short-lived as he soon said even ruder things about them.

Fr. Bruce Cornford, the vicar of St. Matthew's, Southsea, wrote in his magazine *The Gadfly*: 'Scots, Irishmen, Welshmen, Atheists, Agnostics, Dissenters, Parsees, Protestants and all manner of men crowded the negative lobby, where they were wrongly counted like a herd of pigs—and returned to their seats to tell Catholic Christians how they were to say their prayers'!

He was always a stormy petrel for when he was a curate in Southampton he was so angered by his vicar's long and frequent holidays that he put the vicarage up to be sold while he was away. The vicar returned very rapidly and gave him the sack for his pains.

When Archbishop Lang was appointed to Canterbury, Bruce Cornford wrote in his magazine: 'I do not think he is a fit and proper person to be Archbishop; as for leadership, he couldn't lead the Mothers' Union across Southsea Common.'

All these things passed me by and I could not think what all the fuss was about except that to judge from the noise Anglo-Catholics were making we were being persecuted—as I was led to suppose we always had been—and I was already enough of a party man to express abhorrence of the 'New Book'.

What in fact happened was that an era of complete liturgical chaos was ushered in and is still with us, having extended to the Holy Roman Church, which today appears like a lady in very old-fashioned clothes who is trying to turn a somersault.

At Cranleigh we used the Prayer Book and sang Matins and Evensong every Sunday with a slightly shortened version on weekdays. I never remember boys resenting this much, it was just accepted as part of our common life. We did everything —eating, sleeping, learning and playing—at the same time and it seemed perfectly natural that we should worship God together.

These days boys at public schools are in a ferment about compulsory chapel and regard it as the grossest infringement of their liberties. I sometimes think that the answer would be to put the chapel 'out of bounds' and punish boys severely for going there and then they would feel deprived and want to go to church for the rest of their lives!

I had learned enough about the Catholic religion to know that Mass on Sundays was an obligation and so on my first Sunday at school I discovered it was at eight o'clock and I got up early and attended. This was thought by my fellows to have been a mistake and caused great hilarity as a 'new boy' story. I was stopped in the corridors by senior boys from other houses who asked, somewhat crudely: 'Are you the little tick that went to early breakfast?'

I was not confirmed and had not made my communion, but the service had been something of a surprise to me for I had become so used to vestments that the surplice and stole appeared rather *outré* and I was puzzled by the fact that all the clerical members of the staff were in the sanctuary and hopped up to read the epistle and gospel. On writing to my mother later in the day I said that it had been a sort of Low/High Mass and they had all worn very long cottas.

My presence in chapel had been observed by the headmaster and he sent for me and told me kindly that I was not expected to attend. He also said he thought that I ought to be confirmed as soon as possible and he would get my housemaster to write to my parents about it. I am now quite convinced that I ought to have been confirmed much earlier as I had developed a great devotion to the Blessed Sacrament by the time I was nine years old, but in those days bishops made a great fuss about the age of those they confirmed and made very stringent regulations about it.

Fr. Pat Shaw of York, when asked to supply the ages of his confirmation candidates added their weight and height implying that this information seemed to him as relevant to the administration of the sacrament as their age. It was he who when showing Queen Mary the marvellous medieval glass in his church said, as they passed in front of the tabernacle: 'This is where we bob, ma'am,' and she did.

The Headmaster of Cranleigh took very little part in my preparation for the sacraments except for a private interview on the night before the confirmation, when he asked if I had any problems and gave me an obscure warning about older boys which I did not yet understand. As I was too awed to say anything he told me to kneel down beside his chair and I was very conscious that he had spilt egg down his waistcoat.

After a short prayer he asked: 'What do they call you at home?' Even at that solemn moment my perverse sense of humour made me think that I might give a very unexpected reply! However I resisted the temptation and he put his hands on my head saying with emotion: 'God bless you, Colin.' This was a rare privilege as he normally called us all 'lad', which even then had a somewhat archaic flavour.

The main work of my preparation was entrusted to the headmaster of the preparatory school who was also in Holy Orders. He was a deeply religious man and definitely high church with a sister who was a nun at Wantage and a cousin who was a monk at Mirfield. Like many schoolmasters of his day he had a rather puritanical outlook on sex and an unhealthy interest in corporal punishment—he once caned the entire junior school. At night he would creep round the dormitories with a torch looking for boys who were masturbating and on suspicion would drag them out of bed there and then to belabour them with a clothes brush which he had christened 'Charlie'.

To be fair, these things were told me by those who had been at the prep school and I did not experience this side of him myself. With me he was always kind and patient and constantly surprised at my precocity for I had picked up a lot of odd information from the R.C. tracts of which I was so fond and I knew far more about ceremonial than was healthy. I had in fact begun with the jam—a fault which has reappeared in other departments in my life.

I think he realised that I was genuinely more interested in religion than most of my fellows and he took a lot of trouble to bring me into a living relationship with God and for this I can never be grateful enough.

He attempted to moderate my devotion to the Blessed Virgin and warned me against the doctrine of the Assumption, which he obviously did not understand, so I whipped out a little pamphlet and tried to put him right; but I discovered that he much preferred to think that Roman Catholics taught that Our Lady did not die but just shot up into the air, an opinion which the pious picture on the front of my tract certainly reinforced!

In the course of my instruction for confirmation he suggested that I might like to make my confession and as his cousin, a member of the Community of the Resurrection, was coming to stay with him the following week, this would be a good opportunity for me to do so.

It was strange that he should not have arranged to hear my confession himself; he may well have seen the wisdom of having an external confessor in any closed community. Boys from one of the Woodard Schools seriously believed that some of their fellows had been expelled after going to confession. Yet I rather suspect that it was a manifestation of a strange unprofessionalism on the part of the Anglican clergy, many of whom entirely agree with confession and make their own, but have never got round to learning how to administer the sacrament themselves.

Of course at Cranleigh confession was not a usual exercise. Canon C. W. Hutchinson (the beloved 'Hutch') who was the school missioner for some time told me that shortly before I arrived he had been preaching at the school and the headmaster said to him : 'Would you be prepared to hear confessions?' and added ominously, 'There are some boys who are going to be expelled.'

He spent a lot of time in the chapel and was surprised at the number of boys who came. Next morning when he came to breakfast in the Masters' Common Room he was immediately aware of the atmosphere which was heavy with disapproval and he realised that the staff were furious at this interference.

I went over secretly to the chapel of the junior school having worked my way through the self-examination questions in the little St. Swithun Prayer Book which at that time was my standard and authority of all that was correct. I seemed to have done everything and might well have been like the small boy who read right to the end and confessed he had 'been published and printed by the Church Union'!

This was to be my first meeting with an Anglican monk and I was not disappointed for Fr. Eustace Hill C.R. was an impressive figure by any standards. Immensely tall and ascetic-looking in a black cassock with a crucifix at his waist, the first thing of which I became conscious was that he only had one arm. As a chaplain in the Great War he had been shot at point blank range by a German officer when he refused to obey an order on being taken prisoner. Those who witnessed the incident reported that he stood unmoved, with his arm bloody and shattered, saying in a voice of thunder : 'I am a non-combatant. Couldn't you see

43

the cross on my shoulder?' while the German visibly quailed before this terrifying figure.

He was not frightening to me and knew his job as a confessor. I read out my list of sins and he appeared to be quite unmoved and indeed quite uninterested in those which had given me the deepest heart-searching as to whether I could possibly reveal them. He talked a bit about my prayers and then gave me a long lecture on (of all things to a schoolboy) the iniquity of birth control.

I can honestly say that I had not the least idea what he was talking about, but he did not leave it there for he sent me through the post some anti-birth-control pamphlets which I was showing around to other boys, older and more knowing than I was, when a prefect saw and confiscated them. This led to an interview with my housemaster who, realising my ignorance, gave me a talk which made things rather clearer but frightened me very much.

Birth control was a mania with Fr. Eustace who had worked in South Africa where his imperialist heart had been deeply shocked by the sight of Boer families increasing while the British were obviously limiting theirs. He campaigned about it in the most unlikely quarters, as I had discovered, but finally came to think that the Church of England had compromised itself too deeply in this matter and decided he must make his submission to Rome, which seemed uncompromising on this issue. How he would have applauded Pope Paul!

Nothing would convince him that his Orders were invalid and he explained his action by saying: 'I'm a cricketing man and I know that when the umpire says you're out you go out. I know perfectly well I'm a priest, but the Pope is the umpire and I'm perfectly prepared to abide by his decision.'

As an act of reparation he became a lay-brother in a very austere community, but continued to say Morning and Evening Prayer in his cell and, when writing to his old friends, always referred to the Roman church as 'they'.

It was not only Anglo-Catholics who felt strongly about birth control at this time for the Bishop of London wrote that he would like to make a bonfire of all contraceptives and dance round it.

At the end of my confession I experienced such relief that I can remember running down the hill from the junior school and several times jumping in the air from sheer light-heartedness. Since then I have been to confession thousands of times and had some very odd experiences as is the lot of any member of the Church of England who moves around a bit; but it has never again brought me such a feeling of physical well-being.

Once in the big kiosk-like confessionals at St. Bart's a deaf old lady came and knelt on top of me and the priest had to come and haul her off.

Another memorable occasion was when I ventured to go to Prebendary Mackay at All Saints, Margaret Street and he sat up very straight-backed behind the altar rail wearing pince-nez and a face of such severity that I completely forgot what I had come to say. Yet he was one of the greatest priests of our time.

I remember a Cowley Father barking: 'That is a most serious sin', when I said that I had not gone to Mass having intended to do so the night before. I ventured to say: 'It was not a Sunday, Father', and he bellowed: 'Don't try to justify yourself to me, Sir.'

I once said to a strange priest who was obviously not used to hearing confessions: 'You haven't given me a penance, Father', and he replied, 'Make yourself a living sacrifice.' I left the confessional so puzzled that I went to another priest to ask what I should do and he said: 'Nonsense, say three Hail Marys.'

Yet in spite of all peculiarities I have always found that the use of the Sacrament of Penance is some sort of a test of my sincerity, and an outward expression of a desire to please God at some, if only a small, cost.

On the morning of my confirmation I awoke early and said all the prayers I could find in my little St. Swithun—including those for a Good Death. I remember little about the confirmation or my first communion, but I already had a great awe of the sacrament and this was deepened. My parents attended the service and took me out to a good lunch afterwards. In the afternoon we visited the studio of G. F. Watts, the Victorian painter at Compton and looked at his famous picture of Hope sitting blindfold on the world holding a harp with broken strings.

It was not long before I got myself made a chapel server for the senior member of the fraternity was in my house and was a particularly dirty-minded boy who used to make lewd gestures in the sanctuary with a deadpan face when he thought the masters were not looking. He was reputed to drink the communion wine 'on the quiet' which I discovered was true as he invited me into the vestry to have a nip which I was much too prudish to accept. I knew far more about churchy things than he did and very soon he retired gracefully and I took his place, becoming recognised as a great authority in this arena of school life for the rest of my time at Cranleigh.

There was a school chaplain who also taught biology and was said to be a modernist. I had not the least idea what this meant except that in Anglo-Catholic circles it was spoken of with great disapprobation and I was not surprised that he did not turn east for the Creed; although I did not know at the time that this was a purely Anglican custom and if he had been a great Romanist he would not have done so either. He seemed to be much more interested in dissecting frogs than in chapel affairs so that I do not remember having much to do with him.

However quite suddenly two of the masters got ordained. I suppose we were told it was going to happen, but it certainly took me by surprise when they appeared in 'dog-collars' and I can remember discussing with one of my friends who else on the staff might quite likely take the same turn.

One of them was rather 'high' and it is a measure of the authority on church matters which I had assumed that when he was priested he said to me after supper one evening: 'I shall be celebrating the Holy Communion tomorrow so perhaps you would come to the chapel and show me what one does.' So with superb self-confidence I showed him what I thought I had seen priests in high churches doing, but I blush now at the memory of the fussy and incorrect things I told him to do. He had a distinguished career in the church after he retired from school-mastering and, although I never saw him say Mass in later years, I hoped very much that someone had taught him better along the way.

He once preached to us about Platonic friendship, in which he was much interested, from the text: 'See that you love one another.' This caused a great stir amongst the house-masters who spent a lot of their time and energy in trying to ensure that we did no such thing. The fact that there were those on the staff who underlined the romantic nature of these attachments and encouraged them to come out into the open meant that Cranleigh was morally better than many other schools at that period where such things were rigorously suppressed.

We had many distinguished preachers, but I do not recall any of their sermons. The gloomy Dean Inge looked on small boys with obvious distaste while Bishop Winnington-Ingram was more forthcoming and pursued us to our dormitories for a pillow fight, which even at that time had become a trifle old-fashioned, and we just did it to amuse him. He also insisted on playing squash and hockey—but those who played with him were warned that he liked to win.

Our new headmaster, who came when I had been there about two years, used to get the sixth form on Monday mornings to award marks for the previous evening's sermon about which he himself was remarkably frank. 'Very appropriate', he said of a visiting preacher who had the misfortune to have the initials B.F.

This headmaster was a great contrast to his elderly predecessor as, apart from being remarkably young for so responsible a position, he was quite uninterested in games and determined to raise the scholastic standards of what was considered a rather 'tough' school. He dutifully appeared on the touch-line, but it was said that he once arrived at half-time, stood for a moment looking at the players standing about and said: 'A remarkably dull game', and walked away.

He was a continual fascination to us for he had very strong likes and dislikes and no inhibitions in showing them. He hated women who wore scent and would clap a handkerchief to his nose drenched in eucalyptus while he marched ahead leaving them to totter behind on their high heels as best they could, which was torture for mothers who had 'dressed to kill'. He liked them best when they talked back and he told us with glee of the parent who when he apologised for all the books lying open around him by saying: 'I'm preparing a sermon', replied: 'And pinching a lot from everyone else, I see.'

It would be difficult to describe his churchmanship but I suppose that the Laudian high church was his spiritual home with an equal dislike of Romanism and Puritanism.

He treated us like adults and expected us to react as such, but we thought him wildly eccentric—unlike Bishop Herbert of Norwich of whom the Sandringham game-keeper, who had taken him out shooting, said: 'He was just like any other gentleman except that he said "bother" when he missed'—our new headmaster said the real thing when he dropped a pile of books which he always seemed to be carrying.

He must have thought that I was a very curious boy with my intense interest in the externals of religion and he did his best to pull my leg in a kindly way; which means that I have spent the rest of my life pulling his—which he greatly enjoys. I remember his picking up a book from my place in chapel and opening it at Vespers of Our Lady and reading out: 'I am black but comely', grimacing and saying: 'I can think of no justification for regarding the Blessed Virgin as a negress.' He certainly did nothing to damp my spirit or enthusiasm and by this time I had definitely made up my mind that I wanted to be a priest.

It was after reading Fr. Dolling's *Ten Years in a Portsmouth Slum* which records his work and, what I regarded as, his unjust persecution at the hands of Randall Davidson (and to think I had recently shaken hands with the monster when, as retired Archbishop of Canterbury, he had distributed prizes at Cranleigh!). I burned with indignation at the way Fr. Dolling had been treated and longed to get into the fight, but the book also gave me a vision of what a wonderful thing it was to bring souls to Christ through the sacramental life of the church and I wanted to have a part in the ministry which this Portsmouth slum priest had proved to be so efficacious.

Considering how militant I felt towards bishops and what a dance I longed to lead them—which I hoped might compel them to burn me at the stake—it is amusing that the temperature had changed to such an extent by the time I was ordained that, try as I might, I have never managed to have a cross word with one of them. I was also naïve enough to think that one only had to show someone a church with six candles and a tabernacle for them to be converted. I began to take the *Church Times* every week and study the lists of services at Anglo-Catholic churches and feel sure they must be thronged—for who could resist such excitements?

I was amused many years later to hear my predecessor at St. Mary Magdalen, Oxford, Fr. Hack, say: 'I haven't taken the *Church Times* for many years. I had young maids in the house at the time and it did not seem a suitable paper to leave around.' I discovered that he disapproved of a correspondence they had printed about birth control. But I followed passionately the events of the Oxford Movement Centenary and was terribly frustrated that I was at school and unable to participate.

I gathered a band of servers whom I tried to make enthusiastic about things Catholic. One became a very evangelical clergyman so I fear the conversion was not very permanent. We saved up and bought a cotta to wear and I was delighted when the music master said with a smile : 'That garment you were wearing this morning had a very Romish cut about it.'

When I became a prefect and more independent in my movements I used to get up early and go to chapel to say Prime and to wrestle with the various forms of mental prayer all so temptingly laid out in the Centenary Prayer Book—which had the imprimatur of Lord Halifax (and what more could any full-blown paid-up member of the Anglo-Catholic party need!).

During the holidays I still went to St. Bart's, but I had made myself a chapel in the loft over the stables at our house in Henfield. It was filled with every pious object I could get together and my sister referred to it contemptuously as 'shrine land'. I burned incense there and sometimes my lady friends, who were more reverent about it, would join me in saying Vespers of Our Lady.

In 1930 I had paid my first visit to the continent as my housemaster took a party to Oberammergau to see the Passion Play. For the first time I saw Catholic churches in Germany and Belgium, but secretly I did not think them as nice as the Brighton churches.

At Oberammergau the Church Union had made arrangements for Anglican priests to say Mass in a carpenter's work-room, and as they were short of servers I went along early in the morning and served Mass after Mass, really feeling that I was 'living it up'. With the perversity of youth I was far more impressed with this than the play, which lasted eight hours. While the chorus droned on for long periods I was thinking of the acid comments which the lady sacristans had made after each Mass about the eccentricities of the celebrant, which had added considerably to the rather unsuitable education in these matters which I was eagerly drinking in.

One of my friends lived near Alton and when I went to stay with him in the holidays I discovered that there was an Anglican abbey just up the road and so at last I was able to visit an Anglican community. I was enchanted by the impressive gate house and the really big church they had built with their own hands; but most of the original members had been killed in the

49

Great War and they did not easily recover from this loss. For a long time they had no priest in the community.

They had developed from a great work done amongst sailors, but it was a little curious to find a Lady Superior buried in their grave yard, which showed that there had been some ambiguity in their origins—although today it would be counted to them for righteousness!

This visit was enough to stir up my monastic fantasies and I was soon outlining to my friend what I would do if I were Prior. Thinking of the Carthusians I said that I would have them in white habits during the day, but change into black for the night office. 'You mean that they would have dirty habits at night', said my friend, making use of a cant phrase to which we were often subjected at school.

This pricked the bubble of my romanticism and we were soon sniggering away, which was far more in keeping with our age than playing monks. However, my early experience at Cowfold haunted me and I took to telling people that I was going to be a Cowley Father. This was probably exhibitionism and intended to shock them, which it certainly did my parents. My father said that he had no objection to my being a priest, but that I ought to do that first before thinking of anything else.

The curious thing was that I knew next to nothing about the Cowley Fathers except that I had seen a photograph of them wearing their funny black hats. These, oddly enough had been chosen by their founder, Fr. Benson, in order that they might be inconspicuous! Having woven a romantic fantasy about them, when I finally made contact I thought them very unexciting compared with the Fathers of my imagination. I really thought in my late teens I knew 'what was what', and that I had climbed to the highest pinnacles of Anglicanism; but I was hot for new ecclesiastical experience.

At Cranleigh the Prefect of the Week used to sit at the high table with the Master of the Week. During one of my periods of duty the Master, who was an Oxford man, started telling me about churches he had known as an undergraduate. Probably I had told him I was going to be a Cowley Father. 'There is an extraordinary church in Walton Street', he said, 'which manages to combine extreme Roman Catholicism with a kind of Moody and Sankey Protestantism.' I at once pricked up my ears and thought: 'That is for me'—and it was.

4
Oxford

IT IS DIFFICULT to write about my first impressions of Oxford for I have spent so many years of my life there and seen the city under so many intimate guises that it is like trying to write about one's first meeting with a lover after many years of marriage, and attempting to separate what one felt at the time from what one found out later.

Oxford was indeed to me a love affair; at one time I did not think we would ever part and it is true to say that I still suffer from the separation, although one thing life has taught me is that it is fatal to try and go back on one's tracks.

I first saw the beloved city when I went up to take an examination to get me into St. Edmund Hall, and the romance of this great collection of medieval buildings, many of them of monastic origin, made an immediate impact upon me. I was given a room in College over the High which was incredibly noisy so that I awoke with a start every time a lorry passed for it felt as if the building was tumbling down.

At first light I got up and dressed as I had determined to go and find the Cowley Fathers—which was not unnatural as I had been telling people for some time that I was going to join them. Seeing a No. 1 bus marked 'Cowley' I got into it, but the conductor was completely mystified when I asked for 'The Cowley Fathers' and finally directed me to a pile of buildings far along the Cowley Road which proved to be a Salesian School. I found my way to Cowley Parish Church and discovered that I had overshot the mark by a long way and that I really wanted the Iffley Road.

I made one more mistake and got myself into St. John's Home and rather nonplussed the All Saints Sister who opened the door when I asked: 'Is this the Cowley Fathers?' Even then I approached along Marston Street, unaware that there was a public entry in Iffley Road, so that the porter was not best pleased at being called to the door and asked if I might see the church. However he kindly took me along a passage where I nearly swooned with delight for there, hanging in a row, were the flat back hats I had thought so romantic and had fancied myself as wearing.

Frankly the church was rather a disappointment. I am not quite sure what I had expected but I think I had hoped to find it full of monks chanting in a dim religious light. Instead I experienced what I have heard described as 'the Cowley chill'; and in those days the Sacrament was not reserved in the open church which shocked me very much.

Mass was being said in a chapel which looked like a long narrow corridor, and several old ladies had turned their chairs sideways and were lying across them as if they were learning to swim. I could not wait to make my communion as I had to rush back for breakfast and the examination for which I had been summoned. I passed.

What finally expunged Cowley from my thoughts was that soon after this I paid my first visit to Nashdom Abbey and this provided everything that Cowley had seemed to lack. It must be remembered that I am writing of the very superficial judgments of youth.

My cousin, Brian Benson, after having served in the Indian Army and been a member of Ben Greet's Shakespearian Company decided to be a Benedictine monk and entered Nashdom as a novice. I never saw him as an actor, but he cannot have played any role which involved singing as he was completely tone-deaf and the monastic choir certainly did not gain a cantor.

Our relatives said when he became a monk: 'Here we go again, this won't last long'; but they underestimated him, for he died as Prior of Nashdom after over thirty years in religion.

I did not see much of Brian when I was young as he was very much my senior and I have an idea that our mothers were not the best of friends for whenever my sister was being particularly disagreeable my mother would say: 'It's Grace Benson all over again.'

I was very glad when Brian asked me to come to his clothing and I suppose I was the only member of the family who thoroughly approved and I believe I was the only one present on this occasion for both his mother and father had died by this time.

The Anglican Benedictines had had a stormy passage for, although they do not claim it in their own pedigree, their origins really go back to Aelred Carlyle and Caldey Island. I suppose it was natural that I should have been fascinated by Carlyle from the first moment I heard about him, because he had done many of the things I had dreamed about. I never met him as through most of my adult life he was living 'under a cloud' in Canada, but I had often spoken to those who knew him well and to some who had lived with him on Caldey. He seems to have possessed enormous charm and an extraordinary power of catching others up into his enthusiasm. Unfortunately he was a split personality and while one side of him was capable of founding and directing a religious community the other side was very unscrupulous and dishonest.

There can be little doubt that in the many tangled reasons he had in leading his community out of the Anglican Communion and over to Rome one of them was the desire to find some other financial source to pay his considerable debts. The Roman authorities were horrified when they discovered their extent, but so much publicity had been given to the conversion of the Caldey monks that to reveal the true state of affairs would have involved a loss of face which they were not prepared to suffer.

I have often wondered if I had been born somewhat earlier and crossed the path of Aelred Carlyle when I was a boy whether I should have answered his siren call to the shores of Caldey, for it certainly seemed like a fulfilment of many of my monastic fantasies.

The few monks who did not become Roman Catholics set themselves up in a house at Pershore in Worcestershire and here several of the monks I later knew at Nashdom began their monastic life in the sort of discomfort that only men can make if they live together.

Fr. de Lara Wilson once told me that as a layman he had gone to study there and the door was opened by Abbot Denys who asked at once without any preliminaries: 'Can you cook?'

and when Lara said hesitantly that he could added, 'Good, then God has sent you.' He found the kitchen in an indescribable mess and at once went out into the town to buy some new pots and pans as those in use were burned beyond any power he had of cleansing them. When he left some months later the Abbot said to him : 'When the history of the Benedictine revival in the Church of England comes to be written it should be recorded that you saved them from starvation.'

The community moved to Nashdom about 1923 and when I first visited them Abbot Denys had just died and had been replaced by Abbot Martin, a nice but rather pompous man who was very conscious of his position as the only abbot in the Church of England. When R.C. abbots retire they take titular abbacies from the ancient English abbeys and call themselves Abbot of Westminster, Glastonbury, etc. When Abbot Martin retired it was suggested that he might return the compliment and call himself 'Abbot of Downside'.

Nashdom Abbey was a great surprise to me as it was not what I expected a monastery to look like but a very grand house, designed by Lutyens for a Russian Princess who wished to have a *pied à terre* near Windsor. Even today if one lifts a pious picture on the great staircase one finds that it covers a plaster roundel of the Princess's head. It is in fact a very beautiful house of lovely proportions and painted white with green shutters, which means that without constant and expensive renovation it can look rather shabby and seedy.

The gardens had a lovely broad walk of chestnut trees now, alas, fallen victims to the woodman's axe. People used to break through the fence to steal the chestnuts and I remember my cousin once saying that he now understood why the early monks went to live in the desert as there wasn't anything there anyone wanted to pinch!

Once inside the front door all my doubts at the secular appearance of the house were immediately dispersed. The porter was dressed in a black Benedictine habit and the entrance hall, from which a wide flight of steps led up to the chapel, was fragrant with the smell of incense, while a rather dramatic picture of the Sacred Heart hung at the head of the stairs.

The chapel had been constructed out of the ballroom of the house and visitors were allowed in a gallery where once the servants had crept in to peep over the edge and watch the

Russian nobility waltzing below. The high altar was an effective baroque construction designed by an architect named Martin Travers who used his considerable talents in transforming many Anglo-Catholic churches into passable imitations of Italian places of worship, except that he worked in papier maché, which cut the cost but rather gave the impression of a stage set.

The services were entirely in Latin and this was the first time I had heard its use in the Church of England but of course it reminded me of Cowfold Monastery and gave the place a feeling of authenticity. I was enchanted when one of the senior monks said : 'That rogue Bishop Frere defiled our high altar by using English at it.' Here, I felt, was the *crème de la crème* of Anglicanism.

All is now changed, for the chapel has been remodelled and the altar, without candlesticks, stands in the midst of the choir while visitors have been promoted to the principal position before it, the monks sitting in tiers on either side like a choral society. The last vestiges of the Latin tongue remain in the Anthemas of Our Lady sung after Compline.

It used to be said that the only Book of Common Prayer to be found at Nashdom was in the library, filed under 'Comparative Religion', but this was untrue, for after my cousin's death I was sent a Prayer Book which had belonged to him and which showed signs of great use. Not that he was in the least in sympathy with the changes in the church and on my last visit before his death he said : 'Vespers still remains a fairly Christian service except that we have a whole chapter of the Bible read to us in the middle.'

He had an amusing ironic pessimism in his wit, and once when the Abbot was in America wrote recording a whole series of disasters and ended : 'I have asked Dom Michael if there is any good news I can send you and he says that at least the cat seems to be well, but I think it's nursing a secret sorrow.' He collapsed and died almost outside the Roman Catholic cathedral in Edinburgh and a priest dashed out and gave him the last sacraments so that he must have entered heaven with a good laugh.

His profession 'twin' was Dom Gregory Dix who left a great mark on the church through his liturgical scholarship but who also had an impish sense of fun. Once at a Priests' Convention at Dorchester Abbey Bishop Carpenter-Garnier made an emotional speech saying that the great problem to be faced was that we must get our priests to use the Prayer Book. A paper was then read on Confirmation and at question time Dom Gregory rose to his feet and said that it seemed to him that the great problem was that we must get our bishops to use the Prayer Book. He then went on to tell how he had prepared some boys in a mental institution, of which he was chaplain, and as the bishop was in the neighbourhood he asked him to confirm them. The bishop came with some illegal book or other which he managed to get away from him and then asked about the hymns : 'There are no hymns in the service, my Lord.'

'What about the hymn before my address?'

'There is no address in the service, My Lord.'

The penny began to drop and the bishop asked : 'Do you mean to say you want the service just as it stands in the Prayer Book?'

'That was my intention, my Lord.'

The bishop thought for a moment and then said : 'Well I suppose as they are mental defectives it doesn't matter.'

Bishop Carpenter-Garnier was furious and said to him afterwards : 'You have completely destroyed the effect of everything I have said'; to which Dom Gregory replied, with that twinkle in his eye which so infuriated those whose leg he was pulling : 'That was rather the point.'

I am not surprised that I found Nashdom more to my intolerant juvenile tastes than Cowley so that I never went for one of those long walks over Shotover Hill during which the dear good Fathers wrestled for the souls of undergraduates.

Of course Nashdom at various times was very much a changing station for Rome and many members of the community made their submission as individuals.

After I went up to Oxford I often took undergraduate friends there and I was once much embarrassed when one of them asked the Abbot : 'Do you manage to keep the young men long?' It transpired that he thought that it was a theological college!

But I have rather jumped ahead for I have not yet recorded my arrival *in statu pupillari* at St. Edmund Hall, Oxford, in the Michaelmas Term of 1934.

St. Edmund Hall which was unkindly known as 'Queen's Backside' as it was sited in Queen's Lane behind that college, is the only survivor of the medieval halls of residence, which were once numerous in the university. Most of the others were absorbed into colleges and lost their identity; but Teddy Hall, as it was known, managed to retain its name and gradually turn itself into a college with Principal and Fellows.

It has an attractive small front quadrangle and the whole place, including the chapel, is rather a college in miniature. It is built on the spot where St. Edmund of Abingdon took pupils in the thirteenth century. When I came up it was a very 'churchy' college and a high proportion of its members intended to be ordained. As I look at a photograph of the freshmen of my year I see the faces of at least one bishop and several archdeacons.

There was a daily Mass in the chapel which was well attended. I once got into terrible trouble for serving while wearing scarlet slippers. This was thought by the Principal to be a defiant gesture of extreme churchiness—which I was known to favour— but was in fact that I simply forgot to change my bedroom slippers. A friend, with a longer memory than mine, has reminded me recently that I was so aggrieved that I threatened to 'go over' to Rome. He was not a believer at that time and says he remembers my reaction as he was so bewildered—as well he might have been; but I don't think I was speaking seriously. And yet my experience has been that many people take that step for equally irrelevant reasons.

As Teddy Hall was so tiny we were only able to have rooms in college for one year of our three and lodgings had been found for me in Bartlemas Road, some way towards Cowley. When I moved in I discovered that there was a church at the end of the road and I went to investigate. To my great delight there were all the signs of Anglo-Catholicism which I had learned to regard as my spiritual home.

As Oxford extended to the east, Fr. Benson, the founder of the Cowley Fathers, had determined that its new residents should have the advantage of high church principles. He had done a good job, for in the parish of Cowley St. John there were the parish church of SS. Mary & John, the mission church of St. Alban, the conventual church of St. John the Evangelist, three convents and five church schools.

I was delighted to find that I was living almost on the doorstep of SS. Mary & John and that evening in Hall I confided my discovery to the freshman sitting next to me and he said rather loftily : 'It sounds rather depressing to me.' We discovered that we both lived in Sussex and he in Chichester. Why I asked the next question I really don't know, but I was by that time in close touch with various 'extreme' clergymen in Brighton and was probably reflecting their opinions which I had heard. I asked ingenuously: 'Do you know that dreadful Dean?' and of course he said coldly: 'He is my father.' I must say that he took it very well, but never let me forget it.

It is difficult to write about my life as an undergraduate and isolate one particular aspect of it, but it is my ecclesiastical interests upon which I am concentrating and they had a rich flowering in the 'city of dreaming spires'. Apart from the College chapel I began to go to daily Mass at SS. Mary & John, whose vicar, Fr. Walsingham-How, was a shy saintly man whose corpse, when he died not long ago, looked exactly like the Curé d'Ars. They had a High Mass at 11 a.m. on all Feast Days and I noticed a small dark undergraduate who always seemed to be serving, so I got myself in on the party and we soon made friends.

His name was Charles Smith, he had already been up at the university for a year and knew all the ecclesiastical ropes. It was not long before we were cycling all over the city while he showed me the form. He gets very cross when I tell people that it was he who made me 'extreme', but he certainly opened my eyes to all sorts of nuances of churchmanship of which till that time I was unaware. He soon disabused me of the idea that Bart's, Brighton was as high as one could go, although my visit to Nashdom had already made me feel that there were more exalted pastures. I discovered that there were only five churches in the British Isles in which one could completely rely on finding the faith without too much soda-water squirted in. They were St. Peter's, Folkestone; St. Saviour's, Hoxton; St. Michael's, Edinburgh; St. Paul's, Oxford, and Holy Trinity, Reading. Of these only the first and last still remain open to keep the light shining.

Having heard about St. Paul's while at school it was not surprising that I soon made my way there to find out what it was like. To open the great doors under the classical portico was to be transported into a church in the middle of Paris, for it was French Catholicism which Roger Wodehouse, the vicar, loved above all things. The great towering image of Our Lady of Victories (which Roger always said the P.C.C. had chosen from an illustrated catalogue) wearing a silver crown at a jaunty angle, the great baroque tabernacle which revolved and turned

58

itself into a throne for Benediction and which had been brought from a bombed church in Belgium, the altar of Our Lady of Perpetual Succour, all these things seemed more authentic than anything I had seen this side of the Channel.

It was always said that a foreign Catholic was taken to see St. Paul's, Blackfriars, and the Pusey House. He was quite certain that St. Paul's was R.C., Blackfriars Protestant and was not sure what Pusey House could be.

I soon understood what the master at school had meant about combining Roman Catholicism with Moody and Sankey Protestantism for Roger was a strange mixture and loved the most debased of hymns while his preaching, which was most eloquent and amusing, always ended with a solemn and fervent proclamation of salvation through the Precious Blood. I once teased him that Cowper's couplet:

'Redeeming love has been my theme
And shall be till I die'

might have been written about him. Nevertheless, when I first began to preach myself the style I tried to adopt was more influenced by Roger than anyone else.

I am so glad that I saw Roger at the height of his power and influence for St. Paul's was never quite the same after he left. Roger's personality worked wonders in what was largely a slum parish and people loved his humour and generosity. Another thing he taught me was to be able to see the funny side of those to whom one ministers and this has been an enormous help in avoiding the neurotic scenes and rows in which some clergy seem to get engulfed.

Roger had a very aristocratic background for he was a Kimberley of Norfolk and at one time heir to the earldom. Yet he was a fervent socialist, although his background often came out in surprising ways as when he said to one of his curates who had overslept: 'You should have more and better servants.' His stepfather was Lord Chancellor and so he just got the living of St. Paul's through that influence in the most old-fashioned and privileged way. As an undergraduate he had seen this classical church which looked Parisian outside, and thought it should be the same inside, and now he proceeded to make it so.

It was a measure of his personality that just before he was

appointed vicar there had been a great fuss amongst the congregation about a stained glass window which depicted a crucifix. Within twelve months of Roger's incumbency they were having Benediction with a monstrance and not making a murmur. It has been my experience with the C. of E. that a priest can do almost anything if the people like and trust him; but, alas, it does not necessarily turn them into Catholics.

Religion was such fun at St. Paul's with very dressed-up processions in May and October carrying a Black Madonna and the Host enthroned upon an outside altar under the classical portico at Corpus Christi. Everything was lightened by Roger's sense of fun and many were the stories which went round Oxford of the 'goings-on' at St. Paul's. A favourite one was that during a procession of the Virgin Roger was enjoying it so much that he said: 'Round the church once again' and an ethereal female voice from the region of the image said: 'Damn!' loudly and clearly. This was claimed as the one authentic miracle of St. Paul's.

Roger had a great gift of harnessing sentiment to the objectivity of the Catholic religion and often there was a soloist in the gallery singing something like Gounod's 'The Holy City' at Benediction while the May Carol was always sung to the jolly tune of 'the Lincolnshire Poacher'! He was an extraordinary mixture for, in spite of his devotion to all things baroque, he was passionately fond of the old-fashioned Church of England and loved going to cathedral Evensong above all things.

I did not really get to know Roger very well at this time for I had only just started going to St. Paul's when he got involved in a scandal which resulted in his resigning. It was a great tragedy for it wrecked his life and his work and a light went out in Oxford when he left. One of the secrets of his charm was that he had never grown up and a person with more guile would not have behaved with the foolishness which led to the charge of indecency brought against him. While under discipline he came to live in the Guest House of a convent near my home and it was there that I got to know him well and to admire the patience and humility with which he picked up the pieces of his shattered life and climbed back to respect and a useful ministry.

Of course having plenty of money made his path easier, but it must have been a great temptation to turn his back on his priestly vocation. Instead he accepted the disgrace in a spirit of reparation and perhaps the man I came to know and love taught me more about the priesthood than the popular and successful Vicar of St. Paul's could have done. The ultimate measure of one's friendship is how much one misses people when they die. Hardly a day goes by without my wanting to share something with Roger which has amused me and I know would dissolve him in that helpless laughter which was his most characteristic reaction to the absurdities of life.

I suppose a church like St. Paul's, Oxford, even with a wealthy and well-connected vicar, would have had a rougher passage if anyone other than Thomas Strong had been Bishop of Oxford. All he asked was that the clergy would not bother him and he would not bother them. Of some row in a church at Maidenhead he said: 'The real tragedy of the whole thing is that the man wants to see me about it.' He hated high churches where they dressed him up in a cope and tried to make him do ritualistic things, but would attend Benediction quite happily at St. Paul's, dressed in a rochet and chimere, saying with mild apprehension to the boy swinging the incense: 'Will it go off?'

Pointing to a card in the sacristy which read: 'Pope's name: Pius. Bishop's name: Thomas' he said with a twinkle in his eye: 'Does that refer to me or to some other prelate?'

Having driven past the church on Corpus Christi when there was a great altar outside under the portico and Roger was carrying the Sacrament—which at that time would have given most diocesans a stroke—he merely said the next time he met him: 'I saw you yesterday. Up to your little tricks.'

I only set eyes on the bishop once, a strange, small, rather piratical than prelatical figure for he latterly wore a black patch over one eye. After a confirmation it is said that he told the vicar: 'Some of your gals were laffing and I know what they were laffing about. They were laffing at my patch.' His memory got worse and worse, like Archbishop Maclagan who tried to confirm the nurse bending over his bed, her white veil stirring some vague recollections. Poor Tommy Strong was to be seen wandering around the Athenaeum in the early days of the war telling people that he thought he had once held a position of responsibility in the Midlands.

It is strange how sophistication takes hold of one's palate and shrimp paste seems delicious until one has tasted caviar. All the

61

other Anglo-Catholic churches in Oxford seemed rather dull after St. Paul's but I went around them with Charles Smith and we enjoyed what they had to offer.

I chose as my confessor a splendid retired priest who helped at SS. Mary & John but confided to me that he thought it high church and fussy, a judgment with which I agreed, although truth to tell it was very like Bart's, Brighton, which until recently had been my standard of perfection.

Fr. Orr had been for most of his ministry Vicar of Whitwell, in the Isle of Wight, where at first he was much persecuted by the militant protestants led by John Kensit, the notorious bookseller who felt he had a mission to harry ritualists. Oddly enough this outside interference rallied the parishioners to the vicar's defence because, although they did not like the services, they were not going to have *their* vicar pushed around by foreigners. Having come to church to protect him from attack they got used to the worship and got into the habit of attending.

Fr. Orr was the first thorough-going 'papalist' I had known and I was fascinated to notice that, during a sermon in which the Pope was criticised, Fr. Orr was calmly raising his biretta at every mention of the name of the Supreme Pontiff. When he died his wife gave me several of his things including a hair shirt saying: 'My husband always wore it before he married me.' I never knew whether she was joking for she was a sweet and whimsical soul. My mother found it amongst my things and threw it away thinking it was a piece of coconut matting, so I had no opportunity of sampling that rather curious form of austerity.

I did not yet know enough to be surprised that such a dedicated 'pope's man' should have a wife. Of course there were a lot of the older clergy who had only taken up their position after 'committing matrimony' (a turn of phrase I often heard later in Anglo-Catholic circles), but there have always been in the C. of E. some priests who are prepared to be ultra-obedient to every dictate from Rome except celibacy; but which of us do not have blind spots when it suits our purpose?

I was already inoculated against the wiles of low church undergraduates who tried to get one to coffee parties which ended in prayer, which we called 'bottoms up', and to take one to St. Aldate's Church on Sundays.

For the high there was the Pusey House, known as the Puseum, where the Principal and Librarians (who spent more time on souls than books) would recommend the Sacrament of Penance to neophytes whom they had wined and dined in their monastic-type premises (for in those days women were not allowed across the threshold). High Mass there on Sundays in the lovely Temple-more chapel was something of a social occasion and the librarians stood about afterwards wearing birettas and looking like fashion plates for 'Anglo-Catholic Congress' booklets, while they greeted us with less heartiness than we would have found at the door of St. Aldate's.

'The Darwell' (as Dr. Darwell Stone, the former principal, was known) a learned, bearded figure, was still around and consulted by everyone in the Church of England like a Delphic oracle. There were many tales about him such as of the undergraduate who told him he had been to see 'The Dolly Sisters' during the vacation to which 'The Darwell' replied: 'That is a religious community of which I have never heard.'

Principals of Pusey House could be rather unexpected in their replies for I was told that the saintly Stuckey-Coles having been given the Last Sacraments and asked by the priest if there was anything he wanted replied: 'No, unless it be a doughnut'!

After High Mass at the Puseum (about which the Principal of my college said: 'I find it quite a pleasant service if one keeps one's eyes closed at the more hectic moments.') Those of us with aesthetic pretensions who had the *entrée* would go to sherry with a don who lived nearby and who would sometimes hold a lump of sugar on a piece of string which he said sweetened the conversation. It was a rule of the Salon that if one was given a glass of Marsala it meant one had gone too far and must not appear again till invited.

Of course there were many parish churches to sample, although St. Barnabas, the first Catholic Revival church to be built in Oxford, was by my time something of a 'has been'; for the days had passed when the residents of North Oxford flocked to this great brick basilican-style church. Men and women were still made to sit on opposite sides and the vicar would hop out of the procession to rebuke a woman visitor who thought she might sit with her husband.

St. Thomas's, where the vicar, a man of great erudition, never rehearsed the servers and then lost his temper with them in the sanctuary. It was never forgotten by the parishioners that he had struck a boy to the ground during the Mass of the Presanctified on Good Friday!

SS. Philip & James, very Sarum, and St. Margaret's close by very western, were the centre of great turmoil at one stage when the vicar of Phil & Jim was making it western and the vicar of St. Margaret's was busy taking off the six candles from the altar and substituting two while introducing Sarum practices so that the congregation opted for a sort of 'General Post' and it really seemed as if it would be more sensible for the vicars to swap parishes and let the people remain in the pews.

What surprises me most, considering the part St. Mary Magdalen's played in my later life is that I never went to Mass there on a Sunday while I was an undergraduate. I often went in to pray before the Sacrament and would find the venerable Fr. Hack reading from the sermons of Dr. Pusey to one old woman who had started her church life as the Pew Opener. He read them rather like the Koran, after Evensong, for if he was in a hurry he would read only a few lines, but sometimes would continue for some time on a monotone. He once said to me: 'Mary Corbett (the Pew Opener) is a very fortunate woman. She is as one born out of due time for she has heard every sermon that Dr. Pusey ever preached.' There are many more stories about Fr. Hack, but they really belong to a different part of my life.

St. Mary the Virgin, which had echoed to the honied tones of the future Cardinal Newman, we always thought dull; but it came alive on Sunday evenings when the Student Christian Movement arranged for some of the finest preachers of the day to sermonise. Here in packed galleries we listened to the forceful simplicity of Dom Bernard Clements and the compelling logic of William Temple, both able to pack any building in Oxford. It is a sad comment on the problems of the church today that these sermons have been discontinued from lack of support.

I fear that I never went inside a low church except to look at it and I am ashamed when I remember taking a notice reading 'No Service on this table' from a tea shop and leaving it on the altar of a protestant church in the Hinksey Road.

There was a less superficial side to my religious life at Oxford and I was drawn into a small group of undergraduates who were trying to deepen their spiritual life and concern themselves about social problems in the context of the Catholic faith. We called ourselves the Fellowship of the Transfiguration and Trevor Huddleston, slightly senior to me, was one of the founder members.

I can remember being taken along to see Fr. Harold Ellis of the Community of the Resurrection, staying at Pusey House, who directed the Fellowship. In the light of a simple reading lamp and wearing a skull cap he looked the model ascetic, which he was in many ways. We used to club together to pay his fare down to Oxford every term and when he got there he gave us hell for he was a great autocrat and any dissent or opposition was smartly dealt with. It was very good for a young man like me who was beginning to become an insufferable 'know all'.

Fr. Harold was one of the great 'old style' Mirfield Missioners and in the vacation he would take us as helpers on his missions. I can see him now standing on a kitchen table in the chancel of St. Cuthbert's Church, Hebburn-on-Tyne, shouting 'O my brothers, O my sisters' and then dropping his voice to a whisper so that the packed congregation held their breath for fear they should miss a word of what he was saying. It was a very old fashioned technique but it had a miraculous effect and several members of the Salvation Army Band were converted and joined the Church. This has always seemed to me a little hard, as they had generously given their services to help with the nightly Procession of Witness, and the withdrawal of the converts, who played key instruments, closed down the band.

We stayed with the people of the parish, mostly miserably unemployed at that time, and visited diligently in the bleak unattractive streets where real poverty reigned. One of our number, now a distinguished professor of philosophy, cornered a young man who had given up church because his girl friend was a Baptist and said with intensity: 'Have you taken this step from theological conviction or from amatory entanglement?'

But times were changing and I went on other missions with Fr. Harold where he whipped himself into a frenzy which scarcely ruffled the waters and very few came forward to renew their Baptismal Vows (which was regarded as an essential sign that the message of conversion had been accepted).

Poor Fr. Harold, he really could not take change in the Church and was always growling about 'Dangers' which he saw everywhere and finally felt that even the Pope had let him down and that he was the last Catholic left in the Community. Shortly before his death when I was on a rare visit to Mirfield he patted an even more senior member of the Community on the back and said to me: 'This old thing used to have the Faith once, you know.'

I can easily date my first visit to Mirfield, which was for a retreat with the Fellowship, because King Edward VIII abdicated while we were there. Compline was sung early and we followed the Community to the room of Bishop Frere where we heard the Abdication Speech relayed on a very ancient radio with an enormous horn-shaped loudspeaker on which hung a photograph of Cardinal Mercier.

By this time I was regarding myself as very knowledgeable in church matters and during the vacation I saw St. Bart's with eyes from which my rose-tinted spectacles were beginning to slip.

One day instead of going there for confession I went instead to the Church of the Annunciation, another Wagner church as tiny as St. Bart's was large, perched on the side of a very steep hill. I fear my reason for going there was that I had probably done something which I did not want my regular confessor to know about—a very reprehensible attitude which showed that I had not absorbed the *anima catholica* as completely as I prided myself I had. However it had an effect on my life for I met the vicar, Fr. Davies, as I was leaving the church and he asked me where I normally worshipped. When I told him he laughed and said: 'I preached there not long ago. It's not a sermon you have but an interval while the wind performers empty their instruments.' Some months ago I should not have thought this funny, but now I could see the point and as I was leaving he said. 'Our High Mass is always over within the hour.'

My experience in Oxford had taught me that High Mass did not have to be quite as long as the choral settings and long processions at St. Bart's had made me think mandatory. As a result of this remark by Fr. Davies, I began going to Mass at the Church of the Annunciation, dropping my mother at St. Bart's and finding myself with three-quarters of an hour to have a drink in one of Brighton's merry pubs before collecting her again!

I liked Fr. Davies very much and as I did not find the new Vicar of Henfield very sympathetic I soon began to regard the

Annunciation as 'my' church and to serve the altar there; for under Charles Smith's tuition at Oxford I had become quite handy with a thurible.

It was a great shock when Fr. Davies, who was a comparatively young man, died suddenly and I found myself in the midst of the sort of ecclesiastical battle to maintain 'the faith' for which I had always longed. It did not prove as exhilarating and rewarding as I had expected.

Fr. Davies had pushed the Annunciation several notches up the ecclesiastical scale and we did in fact more or less have the Roman Mass in English. George Bell, the Bishop of Chichester, who was making an attempt to produce some sort of liturgical uniformity in his diocese, required that the new vicar should conform to the Prayer Book. The vicar-designate refused to give any undertakings whatever and resigned. We gnashed with our teeth and the bishop retreated and made no demands on the next man appointed.

However our new priest felt bound to restore some of the Prayer Book and there was a miserable period when the congregation was split and various people left the church. One of my fellow servers walked out of the sacristy saying that he had come to Mass and had no intention of taking part in the Tudor Communion Service.

The flames were really fanned by an astounding old priest called Fr. Hrauda, who had been assisting Fr. Davies, and after the changes had taken place would groan and cry out 'Jezebel, Jezebel' when the Prayer for the Church Militant was read and, being Sub-Deacon, he went and sat down on the sedilia at the place in the service when he thought the Gloria should have been sung and said it to himself. This turned High Mass for a few Sundays into a farce, until Fr. Hrauda no longer took part and said a private Mass in Latin in a separate chapel under the tower. What he was doing in the Church of England at all it was hard to tell as he was Austrian and once said to us in a sermon: 'A.C. what does it mean? Amateur Catholic; R.C. what does it mean? Real Catholic.'

I was discovering 'papalism' in the C. of E. with some bewilderment because I had always thought it was a great feather in our cap that we didn't have the Pope. Through my connection with the Annunciation I got to know the Warden of Holy Cross Convent, Haywards Heath, and used often to go and serve in the magnificent Convent chapel. He had entirely latinised the community and he even went so far as to try and persuade me not to take Holy Orders in the Church of England, 'the greatest mistake I ever made' he would say.

Impressionable as I was all this nevertheless seemed rather like *Alice in Wonderland* and I might have been more influenced had not Roger Wodehouse been at hand to take the mickey out of extreme papalism with his racy sense of humour.

I once went with Roger to see Fr. Hrauda when he was in a nursing home the Matron of which was R.C. and asked rather sharply: 'Is he a Catholic?' to which Roger replied: 'As a matter of fact he is a Protestant Minister, but don't for heaven's sake tell him that I said so.' I have a feeling that poor old Fr. Hrauda was really one of those unfortunate people who hate to be in-step with anyone and he died as unco-operatively as he had lived, leaving a large sum of money and no relatives and no will. It could not be said that he did no harm for he caused considerable confusion and distress at the Annunication and when he took a retreat for the monks at Nashdom Abbey he ended with an eloquent plea that they should all 'go over' to Rome, which quite a lot of them did, while he made no attempt to follow them.

But I soon had more chance to seeing the 'papalist' position in what was to me a more comprehensible guise. I believe that it was Charles Smith who first saw a letter in the *Church Times* from Fr. Kenrick, Vicar of Holy Trinity, Hoxton, asking who would join him on pilgrimage to walk to the Shrine of Our Lady of Walsingham. We both decided that we would go.

I had first heard about Walsingham when I was at school for my cousin, who later became a monk, sent me a small card from the Shrine which I put in my Bible, but it said something about 'England's Nazareth' and I had never really understood what it meant.

Now I had begun to have glimmerings of what 'Our Lady of this and that' signified, while pilgrimage was just the thing for a medieval-orientated 'spike' who was reading Chaucer in the English school.

At the last moment Charles was unable to go so I joined the party, which consisted of three priests and two laymen, alone. It took us a week to walk from London to the north coast of Norfolk. It was my first experience of East Anglia, where there seemed to be so much more sky than anywhere else in England, if I do not count a holiday at Lowestoft of which my only memory is of getting sand in my eye for the first time, an unprovoked disaster which left its mark on my mind for I cannot have been much more than four years old when it happened.

The weather was particularly good during the week of our pilgrimage and my memory of this later visit is of sun-filled days and long empty straight roads as we headed north-east staying in small pubs and having Mass early in country churches before setting off on a hard day's grind.

One of the priests, Fr. Leonard, was well over seventy and walked every step of the way. His son Pat became Bishop of Thetford and when, many years later, I came to live in Norfolk I was able to say to him : 'It was your father who first brought me to Walsingham.'

Fr. Kenrick wore a cassock and curé hat so that we were not exactly inconspicuous and we were constantly asked—when it was discovered that we were pilgrims—if we had peas in our shoes! As we trudged along the way instead of telling scabrous tales, like some of Chaucer's pilgrims, I was given a good deal of indoctrination into the why and wherefore of papalism which gave me a mild infection which has lasted ever since, so that I find any theory of authority which by-passes the Bishop of Rome less than satisfactory. When Bishop Wand published a book entitled *What the Church of England stands for* a wag said to me : 'The answer to that is "because there's only one seat and the Pope's in it".'

Fr. Kenrick was a dear man with a large humorous face and, surprisingly enough, a wife. He had spent most of his life working in the slums, although he was enough of a scholar to have translated the Latin Missal into that curious volume known as *The English Missal*—much in evidence in the churches where I worshipped. I did not see him often after this pilgrimage, which is recorded on his memorial in Holy Trinity, Hoxton, but I did once visit him there on a Sunday and was surprised to find only a handful of people at High Mass. I was still at the stage when I honestly thought that the externals of Catholic worship were bound to attract crowds. Mature experience has taught me that they are far more likely to drive them away!

If I did not see much more of Fr. Kenrick my meeting with Fr. Hope Patten at Walsingham was the first of many which lasted till his death, at which I was present. He was the young priest who having become vicar in 1921 of a remote Norfolk village which had been a great centre of medieval pilgrimage, succeeded in bringing it again to life, and catching up his parishioners in his enthusiasm he gained their support instead of, as might have been expected, provoking their opposition.

The story of Walsingham as I learned it was a vision granted to the Saxon Lady of the Manor causing her to build on her lands a small chapel representing the house in which the Holy Family had lived in Palestine and which earned the place the title of 'England's Nazareth'; the name which I had found so puzzling when I first heard of it.

When I padded in to the small village of Walsingham on bare feet with my companions—for we had taken off our shoes at the Slipper Chapel—the Holy House had only recently been rebuilt and the image of Our Lady of Walsingham carried in triumph to it from the parish church followed by a crowd of five thousand, a triumph made more piquant from the fact that the bishop of the diocese had ordered it to be removed and probably thought of it being taken away in a van.

The mystery and romance of the whole place completely captivated me. I have made it quite clear that I was a 'sucker' for what I considered the 'faith of my fathers', and here was a place which seemed as if the Reformation had never happened, a medieval-looking village with its pilgrimage Shrine and devout inhabitants pouring down the village street to Sunday Mass in an old church which was exactly like those I have seen on the continent. It is no wonder that when I left I felt it had all been a dream and could hardly wait to return and reassure myself that it really existed.

In the same way I found Fr. Hope Patten enormously attractive. He looked as I thought a priest ought to look, for he was a handsome man with a great presence and dignity, but very reserved and rather remote unless he was making an effort to exert his considerable charm.

The fact that we were the first organised pilgrimage to come on foot to the Shrine meant that we had a very gracious reception from the Restorer (as he liked to be known, for he was very insistent on continuity with the past). We were entertained in the vicarage and I was thrilled by the priestly conversation which dwelt on the tiresomeness of bishops and malignity of protestants.

Here was Fr. Dolling in person, for Fr. Patten had recently had some controversy with his diocesan, and I was passionately on his side. In fact poor old Bishop Pollock, who had only the vaguest idea what the Shrine was all about, behaved with remarkable restraint, but I was at the age of intolerance and to me all Anglican bishops, except those splendid figures who came from overseas dressed as Roman prelates, were potential enemies.

I am not much given to premonitions, but from the first moment I came to Walsingham I was convinced that the Shrine was to play a part in my life. It is interesting that Fr. Patten once told me that as a boy, oddly enough also strongly influenced by the Brighton churches, he had a feeling that one day he would have charge of a shrine of some kind and that when he first arrived at Walsingham he felt at once, 'This is it'.

As I had intended when I left at the end of the pilgrimage, I came back very soon, and often. Staying in the Pilgrim Hospice and pretending to be doing some work as my Schools drew closer, in fact I spent a lot of time gossiping with the devout ladies who had come to live around the Shrine. I soon discovered that they were engaged in an internecine battle of extraordinary acidity. There are to this day some flower borders in front of one house protected by a low wall because a lady of devout piety was convinced that her neighbours, always at daily Mass, were deliberately encouraging their dog to urinate on her plants and kill them!

My time at Oxford was drawing to a close; from what I have written it would seem that I spent all my time in church, but I did go to a lot of parties, rowed for my College and acted with the Oxford University Dramatic Society. In fact there were moments when I thought I might well give up all idea of the priesthood. However when I was at Nashdom and Walsingham I knew that I should never be able to live comfortably with my conscience if I took any other course.

A new vicar had come to SS. Mary & John, for I was back in my old lodgings during my last year. He promptly changed many of the old fashioned high church ways there and caused great clucking in the hen coops. If those who objected thought they could move him by protest they had got the wrong man for he had the temperament of a war horse under a deceptively mild exterior. He later told me that I first attracted his attention when, being the only server who turned up for some weekday High Mass, I managed the whole job, incense and all, single-handed. Before I left the university he said to me: 'In a couple of years time when you should be thinking of a title (as a first curacy is called) I shall be needing a deacon, so remember that I should be glad to have you here.'

So I left Oxford, which is a traumatic experience for most young men, with the prospect that I should return and this cheered me considerably.

5
Chichester

I DO NOT EVER remember talking to a bishop about ordination. I made up my mind I wanted to be ordained, went to a theological college, found a curacy and my prospective vicar told me that the bishop was prepared to ordain me and I should be informed of the date of the ordination. Even then I did not see the diocesan as he was ill and I was made a deacon by the suffragan bishop.

Looking back, in the light of all the palaver there is today with selection conferences and interviews, it all seems rather casual, but every bishop was a law unto himself in the matter of whom he ordained and some made so few requirements that it was something of a joke.

And yet I sometimes wonder whether the priests of today, who have been selected with enormous care and expense, are of so much better quality than those of an earlier generation. Theological colleges for the training of priests were a result of the Oxford Movement and before this a university degree was regarded as sufficient preparation.

By the time I came on the scene there was a wide selection of colleges and I cannot think why I did not go to St. Stephen's House in Oxford, where Charles Smith was already in residence, and which had produced generations of clergymen who buttoned their cassocks with 39 buttons down the front—when a button fell off we speculated which of the Articles had gone! We much despised double-breasted cassocks which we thought a sign of 'moderation' and which we called 'maternity gowns'.

Nor can I understand why the monastic backgrounds of

Kelham and Mirfield did not provide a stronger pull in their direction. I did once look round the latter and was much intrigued by a notice reading: 'Students are forbidden to introduce naked flames into their rooms.'

A friend who was with me when, on passing through Chichester, we went to look at the chapel of the Theological College says that the moment I saw it I said: 'This is where I'm coming.' So I fear it was 'tat' which tipped the scales.

And yet who of my temperament could have resisted that chapel—it had everything that I had come to consider essential to the true faith: six candles on the high altar, a lady chapel and a requiem chapel (we used to call them 'the ladies' chapel' and the 'old souls' chapel') and presiding over all, under a canopy, a very large statue of St. Richard of Chichester which had, I believe, started life as St. Patrick.

The Chapel was *au fond* an old army hut, but it had been decorated in baroque splendour with monastic stalls painted black and gold. How we smiled when singing the office hymn of the Feast of Dedication at the lines:

> 'Many a blow of biting Sculpture
> Polished well those stones elect.'

The ornate decoration was the work of the previous principal, Herman Leonard Pass, a very distinguished convert from Judaism who had been led to baptism through the influence of Canon Wood of Cambridge and Darwell Stone so that an undergraduate paper printed an unkind cartoon with the legend: 'The heathen in his blindness bows down to Wood and Stone.' Although he became an Anglo-Catholic it was his oriental love of splendour which was expressed in the lushness of the chapel and yards of gold lace sewn on to all the vestments.

As Principal of the College it was not only because he had been a Jew that his students nicknamed him Jehovah, for he lived in awesome remoteness and when he left his rooms he was preceded through the college by a manservant opening the doors and proclaiming: 'Gentlemen, the Principal.' He would issue dispensations from fasting or abstinence from his stall in chapel like a medieval pope. It was he who had given the College its very ultra-Catholic tradition, but by the time I joined he had retired to be a Canon Residentiary at the cathedral.

74

He had begun by saying how much he was looking forward to working with his dear friend the Dean. A fortnight later on being asked how things were going he barked: 'As well as can be expected with a congenital idiot in charge.' From then on he did everything he could to annoy the poor Dean, wearing a biretta in the cathedral because he knew it would outrage the Dean's very pronounced Sarum feelings.

Canon Pass, like many another holy person I have known, was strangely touchy and could behave like a devil to those who had annoyed him. He used to come back and sing Mass at the College once a term and bring with him an alb trimmed with Brussels lace, the sight of which, those of us who considered ourselves 'extreme', much enjoyed.

His successor, Charles Gillett, was one of the most completely charming men I have ever known. He had been Dean of Peterhouse, Cambridge, and always said: 'I am the last person who ought to be Principal of a theological college as I never went to one myself.'

He was a tall, graceful man with a face like a very handsome monkey which could be wonderfully expressive. A friend, who knew a lot of the world, once said to me that Charlie Gillett was the only person of that quality he could think of of whom he had never heard anyone say anything unpleasant. He was supposed to be particularly good and patient with difficult young men, which is probably why he never mentioned the fact that I had turned up a term later than expected.

After I came down from Oxford as the time drew closer for me to start the summer term at Chichester I became beset by doubts. Was I really meant to be a priest? Would it be like going back to my preparatory school after having savoured the freedom of Oxford? Could I bear to live alongside 'churchy' young men, for few of my close friends could be so described?

On the day on which I was due to join the College I sent a rather enigmatic telegram saying that it was impossible to come that term. To avoid explanations I disappeared into the blue with no forwarding address.

That night I was on the ferry from Newhaven to the continent with a car and accompanied by one of my best friends who, having just taken the Foreign Service Exam, had a few months to spare. We had screwed some money out of our parents and stayed abroad till it was spent to the last franc.

75

We had no particular plans and drifted over France and Germany seeing all manner of things, many of which were destroyed by the war a few years later. A world exhibition was taking place in Paris and it was dominated by the German and Russian Pavilions which faced each other with a sinister and prophetic militancy.

The Vatican State also had a Pavilion and in it I saw for the first time some of the fruits of the Liturgical Revival which puzzled me considerably. The central altar had no candles and the vestments displayed looked as if they had been knitted out of string, while the chalices were like rose bowls. Knowing nothing but the 'sandwich board' shaped vestments and jewel-encrusted vessels of the Brighton churches I could hardly believe that the things I regarded as low church were being proudly paraded by Rome herself.

I am surprised that I am not more shaken by it—probably I thought it the eccentricity of a minority. Dr. Darwell Stone said to me when I was a curate in Oxford. 'I constantly see pictures of the Pope blessing gothic vestments, but I notice that he always wears Latin ones'; I found this very comforting at the time, but now even the head man has become Kosher.

By the time our money had run out a new term was about to start and I went off to Chichester like a lamb to the slaughter. In fact I was thoroughly bored with doing nothing but amuse myself, quite sure I wanted to be a priest and never had another doubt from that moment.

In the event I loved Chichester Theological College and count my time there as amongst the happiest periods of my life. It was not at all as I expected and we could hardly be accused of taking ourselves over-seriously for we were laughing at something most of the time.

We were all more or less of the same theological outlook which helped to soften some of the tensions which existed in other colleges between high and low. The only difference we had at Chichester was in the degree of our highness and I, of course, at once allied myself with the most extreme group.

A chief butt of our ridicule were the lovers of Sarum ceremonial, such as Dean Duncan-Jones had established in Chichester Cathedral, and who were very intense about it so that it was easy to tease them. We called the vestments they liked

76

'tents', their long surplice 'nightgowns' and said that when they served they held their hands as if they were urinating.

A Roman Catholic recently said to me. 'One of the things the last few years had taught us is not to "poke Charlie" at other people': and remembering my time at Chichester I replied: 'You're not the only ones.' I was reminded of this when the new Roman instructions for the rites of Holy Week laid down that on Good Friday the cross, if wished, could simply be held up for people to venerate in their places. When Duncan-Jones did this twenty years earlier in Chichester Cathedral he was the laughing-stock of the whole Anglo-Catholic world.

Clerical celibacy was another thing that the 'extreme' group were very keen about, and what jokes we had about clergy wives and would refer to the Book of Common Prayer as 'Mrs. Cranmer's little work'.

I am amused by the fact that most of my fellow students who said the worst things about the married clergy are themselves happily married men today, which leads me to suspect that when anyone is violently 'anti' a thing it shows that he has mighty inclinations in the direction.

Some of the clergy I knew in my youth were very intense about celibacy and Fr. Percy Maryon-Wilson would always behave as if the wives of priests were not there—mercifully they usually thought him either deaf or absent-minded as he would wear a beatific smile while looking right through them. He adopted the same tactics if anyone tried to speak to him before he had said Mass. Once staying in Cornwall with a friend of mine who was taking him to church, Percy was sitting in the front of the car while my friend went to shut the gate. He turned to see that the brake had failed and that the car was slowly approaching the edge of the cliff and was only prevented from going over by a tree. Percy sat staring ahead of him and never said a word. My friend recounting the episode observed: 'He might at least have said "Good-bye".'

Fr. Bristowe of Bagborough, one of the great country parish priests, even went so far as to try and persuade clergy-wives to leave their husbands and boasted as a virtue of the separations he had caused. If one was a married clergyman it was very unwise to let one's wife go to one of his retreats!

At the centenary of the College which occurred while I was there, Athelstan Riley, a prominent and aged Anglo-Catholic layman who had a mania about celibacy, spoke after luncheon for a very long time on this subject. His hearers were sharply divided and while some were cheering others were shouting 'shame', to all of which he was entirely oblivious as he was stone deaf. He sat down at last to mingled claps and boos, only to hop up again immediately to say that he had forgotten to mention that in the Eastern Orthodox church you could not be a bishop if you had a wife. The faces of the happily married bishops sitting with him at the top table were a study!

The life we lived at Chichester was fairly monastic. Matins was at 7 a.m. followed by half an hour of mental prayer before Mass at 8 a.m. On all feasts as well as Sundays it was a High Mass with full Western ceremonial. A student who had come from a remote part of Wales where he had never before seen candles lighted on an altar was asked by the Principal how he was getting on with the services after he had been at the College for a fortnight and he replied: 'I like High Mass all right, but I find the Low Mass a bit dull.'

We worked all the morning at lectures or private study and at 12.30 p.m. after Sext we had Intercessions which we took turns in arranging and conducting. It almost became a competition as to who could produce the most *outré* devotions. Often we just recited the Rosary, which made the eyes of the students from Salisbury, who had come over to play hockey, almost pop out of their heads. There was a ghastly little book called *The Raccolta* which described itself as 'A Manual of Indulgenced Devotions' from which we plucked some gems of Roman Catholic piety which had little to recommend them, except of course a whacking Indulgence—whatever good that may have been to Anglican theological students!

We were free in the afternoon till 5 p.m. and in the summer spent a lot of time on the beach at Wittering. I was amongst those who were lucky enough to have a car and I fear we were not very scrupulous about getting back by five when we were supposed to start working in our rooms.

At 7 p.m. we sang Evensong and then had dinner, but by 8.30 p.m. we were supposed to start working again till we gathered for Compline at 10 p.m. after which there was a Greater Silence till after Mass next day. On Saturdays we were free from luncheon till midnight and those of us with cars went far afield in search of amusement. I can remember many a Cinderella-like drive back from Portsmouth or Brighton trying to beat the clock as if the car would turn into a pumpkin. We were never allowed to go into the pubs in Chichester itself.

The student of today would find this order of things very repressive but I cannot help thinking that the discipline was good for us as it did establish certain habits of piety and study. The moment we were launched into parishes we were swamped with activity and looked back on the ordered life of the College with some nostalgia.

On Sundays we began to have practical experience of parish work. Many of the local clergy lost their fears of the high church character of the College when they wanted someone to take services while they were on holiday. In other parishes we worked all the year round. I preached for the first time in Boxgrove Priory where I was warned that the vicar's wife at the organ rattled the stops if one went on too long.

One of the nicest jobs which I had was to take services in the wards of the Infirmary at East Preston and also to visit the casual wards where the shaggy old tramps—as gentle as they appeared fierce—were locked up like prisoners all Sunday for fear they might move on without doing their stint of work, which Sabbatarian principles prevented them from being allowed to do on the Lord's Day. It is strange that we can imagine we are honouring God by such behaviour!

We all admired the Principal very much and he was a great example to those training for the priesthood. He said Mass with extreme recollection and was obviously a man of prayer. He appeared vague and was indeed very absent minded—he was once seen walking down the street in an overcoat but no trousers, having forgotten to put on his cassock, which the biretta on his head clearly showed he had intended to do. Yet he knew everything that went on in the College and was not fooled for a moment by the deceptions we thought we were getting away with.

His rebukes were always mild and framed in the plural: 'We must try and be more punctual . . .' but he could be very firm and was insistent that the clergy could at least have good manners.

The other members of the staff were a study in contrasts. The Vice-Principal with all the quaint charm of an Irish leprechaun, the Chaplain straight from his first curacy and full of giggles and fun, the Tutor much cleverer than anyone, but almost incredibly disorganised. They could hardly have been less alike but they combined to form a very good team.

They had a lot to suffer from us for we were a very curious bunch. I remember the Chaplain trying to teach us to say Mass and being nearly driven mad by a student who asked repeatedly : 'But suppose the Blessed Sacrament was exposed and a Greater Prelate sitting in choir?' During my time there was an inspection of the College and in the report it was said that we were a lot of very narrow-minded and intolerant young men and that the training we were given was likely to press us into a single mould. I'm sure we were narrow-minded and intolerant, but that is a prerogative of youth; however, thinking of my contemporaries, it was a rather feeble mould which could form such completely different products.

At I look at a College photograph of us wearing cassocks, which we did all the time except at recreation, I realise we have all gone along very different paths. At least two are Roman Catholics, two have committed suicide, one has been to prison, but most of the rest have now settled into every variety of churchmanship—except perhaps conservative evangelical.

I had been simple enough to think that one learned theology at such an establishment, but there simply was not time to do more than scratch the surface and I always regretted that I did not read it at Oxford.

Bishops used to talk pompously of the tradition of 'sound scholarship' in the Church of England not wishing to face the fact that it vanished years ago. They now build new parsonage houses with a vicar's study of a size which could house about three paperbacks—which shows that the clergy are no longer expected to have any books.

I became one of the Masters of Ceremonies at the College and can remember contriving a canopy of four white poles, a length of brocade and brass door knobs. It was carried over the Sacrament on Maundy Thursday and I felt that I had struck a great blow for the faith.

The ceremonies of Holy Week were carried out in the church of St. Bartholomew which was close to the College and is now its chapel. The vicar in those days said : 'I try to put on one new thing each year.' He did and lost part of his congregation each time.

During the College centenary when many old students returned, altars were put up in every part of the buildings and one came out of one's room to find a priest saying Mass at the end of the passage, genuflected, and hurried off to the bathroom.

The High Mass for this great occasion was held in the cathedral and there was some dispute with the Dean over the rite to be used as he was devoted to Sarum ritual and the 1928 Prayer Book, a work which was still regarded as anathema by certain sections of the church. The problem was resolved by the bishop consenting to sing the Mass himself and use Western ceremonial.

One cannot help feeling that he rather enjoyed tormenting the Dean in this way as, like most cathedral closes in England, a Trollopian battle was constantly being waged, the balance of power being in the hands of the Archdeacon who would every now and then change sides and join the Dean in defeating the Bishop on some issue. The rage of the Dean was the greater as it was the first time the Bishop had worn a chasuble in the cathedral, having previously refused to do so at the dean's request.

Duncan-Jones, the Dean, was not a man to disguise his feelings and looked like thunder, but then the College with its 'Romanism' was a constant source of irritation to him and I never remember him crossing its portals.

George Bell, the Bishop, was a bigger man than any of us realised at the time and regarded as something of a saint by the Confessional Church in Germany. He would often come to dinner at the College arriving in time for Evensong and we always thought he peeped into a Roman Calendar as he seemed to choose the eve of some feast such as St. Joseph or The Sacred Heart and showed an amused surprise at the Solemn Evensong he found taking place. He had a prodigious memory and although I had little contact with him would say: 'Ah yes, your father was churchwarden at Henfield,' whenever we met.

Charlie Gillett suffered very much from nervous dyspepsia and was absent for a whole term while I was there. During the war he led the remnant of the College first to Cambridge and then to Edinburgh joining with what was left of Ely and Coates Hall. When the war was over things had changed in the Church for the Central Advisory Board for the Training for the Ministry had been set up, which meant that colleges like Chichester lost a lot of their independence. Charlie did not feel strong enough to return to Chichester and start a battle which he knew would be ultimately lost and so resigned and most of the contents of the chapel were disposed of, except for St. Richard which the butler hid under his bed like one of the faithful during the iconoclastic controversy in the Early Church. Under the new régime the students used the Bishop's chapel so the character of the worship was considerably changed. However I am glad I was there before the war and saw it as it was in the last sunset glow of the baroque.

Charlie went first as chaplain to some enclosed nuns and then lived in the Clergy Houses of St. Bart's, Brighton and Little St. Mary's, Cambridge, but he was rather a sad figure for he was a lonely man, a great priest, a considerable scholar and he was very much wasted.

During my second year at Chichester the threat of war began to appear on the horizon. The events leading up to Munich came as a great shock for, having grown up in the years after the Great War, I fully believed that another conflict of that sort was impossible. As in the panic of the emergency we filled sandbags at the local hospital, it seemed that the whole situation was a bad dream and I rejoiced as much as anyone when Neville Chamberlain claimed to have gained 'Peace in our time'.

It is extraordinary that in the year after Munich most of us came to accept the idea of war as inevitable. I can remember during this time going to tea with friends at Fullers almost every afternoon and talking gloomily about the future. We stuffed ourselves with iced walnut cake not only because eating is a well known psychological alternative to drinking as relief from worry, but because we thought such delicacies would soon disappear when war began—and how right we were!

I had fixed to go to SS. Mary & John as a curate and the Bishop of Oxford was prepared to accept me for ordination as I had passed all the necessary examinations. No one seemed to know at that time whether or not ordination candidates might be called up for military service, for the mobilisation act only exempted 'the blind, the insane and ministers of religion'; and we did not yet exactly qualify under any of those headings! Life itself seemed fairly uncertain for we were all convinced —although we knew nothing then of the horrors of the atomic bomb—that the war would begin with a great holocaust.

There was a German student, an ex-Lutheran pastor, at the College and one morning the police came for him while we were having High Mass at which he was acting as Sub-Deacon. They stood at the back of the chapel with their caps in their hands till we had finished the Mass. We were all very upset when he was taken off for internment.

My ordination as a Deacon was fixed for September 23rd, 1939 but there was more than one area of uncertainty as the Bishop of Oxford had suffered a breakdown in health.

On the first Sunday in September I was to conduct Matins at a small village in the heart of the South Downs. When I got there I found a note pinned on the door saying that in view of the Prime Minister's speech the service would begin late. I went to the house of one of the churchwardens who was a retired admiral and listened to the very depressing news that we were at war with Germany. The admiral was in a high state of excitement rubbing his hands together and longing to get at the enemy.

Like many other people, I had been expecting England to be involved for so long and by this time had such a guilty conscience about Munich that in some ways I experienced a sense of relief that it had happened at last.

We went over to the church and began the service, but while we were singing the Te Deum an extraordinary figure in a tin hat and gas mask appeared at the door and loudly blew a whistle shouting 'Air Raid Warning Red'. It was what we had all been expecting and panic was complete. The man pumping the organ stopped at once and the music ended in a whimper while the whole congregation shot off to shelters or air-raid stations. No one thought to enquire where I was to shelter and I remained alone in the church, writing in the register : 'Service abandoned owing to air-raid warning', which I thought might fascinate future generations if we survived. Everything was looking particularly peaceful as I drove back to college but I think we all sensed that things would never be the same again.

There had been a fever of activity for the protection of our country and people started constructing road blocks made of tree trunks with a bicycle wheel on the end so that they could be quickly put into position and supposedly stop a tank, which even at that time I thought a little ridiculous.

As no one knew what was likely to happen it was decided

that I should go off to Oxford at once and settle into the parish, which was being flooded with children evacuated from London. As in the gospel precept, I did not turn back to say farewell to father or mother, but packed my bags and left Chichester with a heavy heart.

The weather was perfect as if to make the disruption of ordinary life more agonising and as I drove to Oxford I thought that I had never seen the countryside looking more lovely and tranquil. It was hard to realise that we were preparing to fight a war.

6
Cowley St. John

THE ORDINATION RETREAT was held at Christ Church as the college chapel is also the cathedral of the Diocese of Oxford.

In the autumn of 1939 the place was full of mothers and children who had been evacuated from London. The ordinands sat in the great hall at meal times, a single table of black figures, but the mums had seen so many new and strange sights that they did not appear to notice us.

The ordination was taken by the Bishop of Dorchester who was known as 'Puffles', for Bishop Kirk, the Diocesan, was ill. 'Puffles' was a sweet kind man and I loved him dearly; but he had absolutely no sense of the ridiculous and always managed to make ceremonies a little hilarious by trying too hard to be dignified.

He had several clichés which he always brought into his sermons. One of these was to hold up his hands and say: 'These hands unworthy, but commissioned.' A friend of mine one day came upon him cleaning his nails and he looked up and said: 'Consecrated hands, however unworthy, should be clean.' My friend laughed thinking he was making a joke—but he was not! Yet no one could have been kinder to those in trouble nor had a more pastoral heart and he wore himself out in the service of others.

The ordinations at Christ Church, since Kirk had become Bishop of Oxford, set a new liturgical standard which has since been copied by other dioceses, but at that time it was a novelty to see an Anglican bishop in his own cathedral wearing all the traditional vestments, including gloves. All my youth I had seen bishops from overseas in all this episcopal pomp at Anglo-Catholic churches in London but it seemed wonderful to see an English diocesan behaving in this way. Kirk was a great scholar, but it was only after he became a bishop that he displayed his taste for ritualism and paid little attention to the usual Anglican taste for moderation.

He went around the diocese in a biretta and wore a cappa magna on occasions. When I was Vicar of St. Mary Magdalen he came to preach wearing a rochet of Brussels lace which got caught up in the pulpit. I could not help thinking that if in my 'extreme' youth I had been told that I should live to disentangle the Diocesan's Brussels lace I should not, for all my powers of fantasy, have dreamed it to be within the realms of possibility.

I was very worried that I might have a sick headache on the day of my ordination for any excitement gave me what I thought was a liver attack, but discovered many years later was migraine. I therefore took twice the maximum dose of Carter's Little Liver Pills the night before on the principle of making doubly sure, and felt fine—if a little flatulent—next day.

That night I sat for the first time in a priest's stall at SS. Mary & John's while Solemn Evensong was sung, very conscious of the brand new biretta on my head (what a party symbol it was) which I took on and off every time the Gloria was sung or the Holy Name mentioned. I would have found it hard to believe that the day would come, as it has, when I wouldn't know where my biretta was if I wanted it.

When Fr. Benson had bought the site on which the church of SS. Mary & John was built he determined to keep a night vigil of prayer. He was arrested by the police who thought he was a tramp up to no good. He had built a splendid, large church very handsome in its adornments but oddly enough when one considers its origin in prayer and the really holy people who had worshipped there, it never seemed to me to have much atmosphere.

In this it was so unlike St. Mary Magdalen, where I was later vicar. Of course St. Mary Magdalen was a much older church but often when I opened it in the morning it was so full of a feeling of life that I found it hard to believe that I was alone in the building. Whereas at SS. Mary & John I often went into the church half an hour after it had been packed for High Mass and, apart from votive candles burning and the smell of incense, it was difficult to feel that anyone had been near the place.

It had become an enormous parish in a tightly built-up area and with five schools and three churches there were so many ramifications that there was almost always a crisis of some sort.

One of the churches was that of the Cowley Fathers, which was extra-parochial although it drew its large congregation mainly from the parish. This reproduced one of the great medieval causes of friction between the religious and secular clergy and it was strange to see history repeating itself in this way.

The Cowley Fathers were the patrons of the living and so had appointed the vicar and naturally each one came as a great friend of the Community. It did not take them long to become quite violent about the poor Fathers who they felt were poaching in their parish and taking money from the few wealthy old ladies who lived there.

My vicar was no exception and part of the weekly staff meeting was devoted to a recital of the iniquities of the 'monks down the road'. I think my vicar really rather enjoyed having rows and usually had one or two on hand which he pursued with enthusiasm and a certain relish. He had been domestic chaplain to Lord Halifax whose family were quite sure that the old Earl also enjoyed the periodical disputes he had with his chaplain.

It was the time when the Anglo-Catholic priests around Hickleton, where Halifax lived, in Yorkshire were known as 'The Black Hand Gang' and would foster this impression by meeting in secret conclave and making good use of the influence of their patron.

I suppose Halifax is the perfect example of the wealthy high church layman who has today almost disappeared from the ecclesiastical scene. He even took a chaplain with him on his honeymoon and for the Oxford Movement Centenary in 1933 when he was a very old man had a great altar pavilion designed and built in his garden at enormous cost for a single High Mass. It is said that if you were staying at Hickleton you were called in the morning by the butler who said : 'Tea or Eucharist, Sir?'

Another like him was Sir Hubert Miller, the squire of Froyle, who was known by his family as 'the Church Milliner here on earth'. To mark his twenty-first birthday he presented Lower Froyle with a Mission church dedicated to St. Joseph and during his long life he brought back from Italy many things to embellish not only the church but the village, for the parishioners were made to have statues of saints over their cottage doorways. He himself used to act as Master of Ceremonies and produced a rod of office as used in Italy to point delicately to the place acolytes were to occupy. Sir Hubert got so enraged with his rustic servers that he began using it to give them a sharp thwack, not even sparing the Sacred Ministers when they were slow on the uptake. He became more peppery in temper as he grew older and reacted violently when he asked a priest his name and was answered : 'Whye'—which was indeed his name. 'It was a perfectly civil question', barked Sir Hubert who would listen to no explanations.

More gentle was Sir Alfred Joderell of Bayfield, Norfolk, who liked to be known as the Lord Halifax of East Anglia, and spent large amounts of money putting marble reredoses into churches on his estate.

Much in the Halifax tradition was the Duke of Newcastle who maintained a choir who sang Evensong at the great church at Clumber on his Nottinghamshire estate.

Last in the line and gentlest of all was Sam Gurney who transformed the tiny church near his house in Berkshire into an Anglo-Catholic paradise and persuaded the villagers to carry from his bedroom—where it was usually kept—a life-size statue of St. Swithin in honour of their parish feast. He loved presenting things to churches and the Chapter of Norwich Cathedral were surprised to be offered a large Spanish Confessional box which they declined with thanks. When Sam died in 1968 it seemed the end of an era for there are few today who have either the leisure or the money to give themselves so completely to churchy interests.

My vicar, Hal Painter, was a perfectionist and I am enormously grateful to him for his fussiness. He said constantly that any slackness in the sanctuary would be reflected in one's work throughout the whole parish and he insisted that everything was done to the last degree of correctness. In those days it was possible to know to the least movement of one's hand what was and what was not correct. The idea behind it was that one became entirely impersonal and was just any priest performing a rite. An undergraduate who had never been to High Mass before and saw us moving about the sanctuary with expressionless faces said to me afterwards: 'I have never seen three more snooty-looking buggers in my life.'

When I first began saying Mass I sometimes felt that I was doing it in a shop window, for if I put my hand slightly in the wrong place I would hear the vicar give a sharp intake of breath and would guiltily move it. This was excellent training for, by the time I left the parish I knew how to say Mass correctly without having to pay attention to the externals.

Now all has changed—I once said that I wished I didn't know what one was supposed to do as I found the way some priests said Mass so distracting. God seems to have answered my prayer!

There were five of us on the staff and we looked like French clerics when we all went out together in soutane cassocks and round beaver hats. The Senior Curate, who was called Tommy, was pathologically shy and had a great distaste for parish work, spending most of his time typing out lists and playing the piano. He was once seen slipping down a street in his district popping cards through the letter-box saying he had called, but in fact the bell remained unrung!

The Priest-in-Charge at the daughter church, which had been built far too close to the parish church, was Billy Favell, the most urbane of clergymen who lived with his adorable mother in a hideous little brick house which had a hall attached. It was in fact a palace and a cathedral for it had been built by a curious *episcopus vagans* who claimed to be Bishop of Mercia. It was always said in Oxford that one must talk to him with one's hat on or one was liable to find oneself rapidly ordained into his diocese.

When Fr. Hack was vicar of St. Thomas, a wandering bishop set up in the parish and Hack gave out in the notices 'a gentleman who calls himself Bishop James has come to live in Hythe Bridge Street. I would like to make it clear that he is not in Communion with the Church of England, he is not in Communion with the Church of Rome and as far as I know he is in Communion with no one either in heaven or on earth'.

The 'palace in Percy Street was an ugly house, but Billy's mother had made it exquisite inside with thick carpets and nice furniture. They were both most hospitable even under war-time restrictions and I found their house a wonderful refuge when parish life got too intense.

Staff meetings were apt to be fraught with tension as there was always some crisis in progress and the curates sat holding their breath until discovering what mood the vicar was in.

We taught almost every day in the schools and I was given a special responsibility for the Infant School. The headmistress liked me to give them a little talk after prayers and she would turn to me and say with the sweetest of smiles: 'Will you say just one word, Father?' I often wondered how she would have reacted if I had fallen on one knee and said 'Dora', which was her Christian name. When I was priested she said to the children: 'You can now call Father "Father" and mean it because he is really a Father now.' They looked at me with innocent eyes, but some of them were more sophisticated than she thought and one little cherub came up to me afterwards and said: 'Who had the baby?'

Of the four convents in the Cowley St. John district one was the Magdalen Road Mission House where our parish sisters lived. On his arrival Fr. Painter had said that there must be younger sisters, as the youngest in the house was well over seventy. Their Order hadn't any younger models available so they decided to withdraw. It was perhaps unfortunate that when writing of this change in the parish magazine the vicar should have mentioned old horses being put out to grass!

Their place was to be taken by Sisters from Laleham Abbey whose redoubtable Mother Sarah came to inspect the house: 'Good heavens, what a state the ceilings are in', she said. The old Sister Superior thrust her hands deeper into her sleeves and replied: 'We never raise our eyes.'

My previous experience of nuns had been the convent near my home where I had acted as a server for some years. Here the Sisters always prefaced everything with: 'May I respectfully ask (or say). . . .' Once when Charlie Gillett was staying in retreat something went wrong with the W.C. A Sister mysteriously led him down a long passage, opened the door of another closet, gave a deep curtsey, and said: 'Father, with deepest respect.'

I loved the Laleham Sisters, but the Sister-in-Charge was rather more temperamental than one might expect a nun to be. She expressed her disapproval by 'sending to Coventry' those who had displeased her. She once refused to speak to me for a month because I had cleared up the sacristy, which was long overdue, while she was away. However after the war when she had had an audience with Pope Pius XII I met her and she told me that he had said he sent his blessing to her nearest and dearest: 'And of course that meant you, Father', she said with a sweet smile which showed that all was forgotten and forgiven.

Laleham Abbey from which the Sisters came was a large house by the Thames filled with objects of piety mostly draped in lace. Mother Sarah had, at that time, taken to playing the harp and she would slip from her stall in chapel and give a run up the strings, instead of a bell, when the Tabernacle was opened. The rooms were called after places in the Gospel and once when I called, the Porteress said: 'Mother is playing the harp in Jerusalem', which for a moment made me wonder if this could be a tactful way of announcing her demise.

At the beginning of the war the monks from Nashdom were evacuated to the Girls' School at Laleham and I went over to see my cousin there. The discomfort was more than their rule required for the rooms had been built for very small girls and the beds were to scale. Here all the rooms had been called after flowers and at night there was some activity as members of the Community crept around transferring the card reading 'Pansy' to someone else's door.

My cousin was one day scrubbing a floor and opening a door threw out the dirty water from the bucket. Unfortunately Mother Sarah was passing at that moment!

Soon after the monks moved to Malling Abbey in Kent which was by then in the battle area and where they were able to do various war jobs. I went there for my cousin's First Mass, for he was ordained after I was, and as all the nuns had been evacuated I was put to sleep in the Abbess's room. Years later I was in a group of people who had all had some connection with Malling and I said: 'I have slept in the Abbess's bedroom.' They obviously thought I was making a joke in the worst possible taste and changed the subject without giving me a chance to explain!

I had hardly got settled in the parish when Fr. Painter, who had been for many years in the Territorial Reserve, was called up as a chaplain. He left looking as immaculate in his uniform as he always did in a soutane leaving his female admirers, and there were many of them, in suitable postures of despair. It was rather an anti-climax when he was posted back immediately as chaplain to the hospital in the University Examination Schools.

He was finally sent off to France, but before he left he gave me a serious talk as he was certain, with some reason, that the Senior Curate would immediately shut down everything he could. I was charged to pull in the other direction and keep everything going. The result was that while still a deacon I had to take far more responsibility that I should have done under normal circumstances. Added to this I became an Air Raid Warden and was often up half the night patrolling the streets. One of my companions in this task was a novice from the Franciscan House in Iffley Road whose name was Christmas. I have often wondered if he persevered in his vocation and became Father Christmas.

After the fall of France Fr. Painter came back to England having only just escaped being taken prisoner by the Germans and, after a series of vintage rows with Army authorities, felt the little he could do in the forces was incomparable to the work waiting to be done in his enormous parish, so he got himself demobilised and came home.

One result of his return was that I had to move out of the vicarage where I had been living with his family, and found myself lodgings rather a long way from the church. My land-ladies were very kind and devoted to me and said to one of the neighbours: 'When you go into Fr. Stephenson's room it's like going into church.'

As I was so far from the church I got myself a bicycle and had it painted bright blue. This was something more than eccentricity as in Oxford to have a bicycle without a padlock was as much use as having a padlock without a bicycle. I rightly judged that if made sufficiently distinctive it would be left untouched. It had other advantages, too, for it advertised my presence in different parts of the parish, like a builder's board. It was less convenient when I wanted to hide my light under a bushel.

Cycling in a cassock had certain difficulties and the skirt of mine always showed signs of having been chewed up in the chain. Once when I was cycling at some speed down the very steep hill in Divinity Road I suddenly felt myself jerked back as my tail got caught. I jammed on the brakes and found that I was completely stuck and unable to move. The only solution was to unbutton the cassock but, being the summer, I had not put any trousers on underneath and I had no alternative but to face the possibility of arrest for indecent exposure!

When Roger Wodehouse left St. Paul's he bought a house in Park Town in North Oxford and came for a couple of days each week. As I had got to know him well in the last three years it was natural that when I came back to Oxford I should see him often and thus it was that I got to know Alex Lawson.

I once knew about Alex's origins, which were rather aristocratic, but I have forgotten and now I should doubt if there is anyone who knows, as he never spoke to me himself on the subject and I was at one time closer to him than most people. Anyway, he was more or less adopted by Roger's mother, Lady Sandhurst, and then came to live with Roger in Oxford and was later ordained. He was a tall, willowy figure with an enormous Hapsburg jaw jutting out. He once swallowed his false teeth which almost killed him. Those who liked Roger's extrovert good nature tended to react against Alex's somewhat authoritarian reserve. Having a fixed idea that people were going to be unpleasant to him he had a slap at them first and in this way made many enemies.

It was, I believe, Basil Jellicoe, when he was at St. Stephen's House, who invented for Alex the title L.G.C. (standing for the Lowest of God's Creatures) and the name stuck. It was most unfair for he was dismissed by those who did not know him as a rather silly, extreme young man. He was in fact highly intelligent and one of the best read men I have ever known. He had a lot of surprising talents and was largely responsible for the flair which made St. Paul's such a special church, but he was seldom given any credit for that.

When poor Roger's débacle took place, Alex stayed in Oxford living in Park Town and acting as curate to Fr. Hack at St. Mary Magdalen. He ruled Roger with a rod of iron and Roger once confessed to me that he was more terrified of Alex's anger than that of any other human being.

He came to play a great part in my life for he always had to have someone on hand whom he could dominate, and for some time I was the willing victim. He took me in hand determined to complete my ecclesiastical education, but he taught me many other things besides for he was something of an epicure and had faultless good taste. If I showed any sign of dissent his Hapsburg jaw would jut out and he would say in icy tones:

'How very wrong-minded'—and that was that. The world was entirely divided into those who were right-minded and those who were wrong-minded and I need hardly say that the right-minded were those who agreed with him.

It was he who insisted that I must recite the Roman Breviary in Latin, provided me with a set, and showed me how to use them. He had a private chapel at Park Town and in it we would recite Matins and Lauds after an excellent dinner served with great elegance. The chapel, I need hardly say, had to be seen to be believed and was dominated by a dressed image of Our Lady, the adornments of which he had made himself, after buying the ancient statue in Munich. The cult and title of 'Our Lady of Maternal Guidance' was also his own invention.

I did not get on very well with the Latin and it was a great burden, but he would urge me along with patience and explain that it was better to recite the correct thing, even if one didn't understand it, than consent to the reduced Prayer Book Office which had been compiled with protestant intent. At this distance of time it seems rather dotty, but Alex was so assured and forceful that I felt it was the right thing.

He was very censorious about those who took the sugar of Catholicism and neglected its disciplines. Most particular about clerical decorum and only doing things which were suitable for a priest, he would never allow me to go anywhere with him unless I was dressed in a black suit with the collar.

It is the more astonishing that later in life, after his health had broken and he had had a tough time in a fenland parish for twenty years, he bought a house in Cambridge on a new estate—where he would have said when I first knew him : 'no gentleman could possibly live'—he seldom dressed as a priest, I never saw him reciting the Breviary and he always had some excuse why he couldn't say Mass.

His parish had been tough because of his strong-mindedness for he made rules and was completely inflexible about them. Only those who attended church regularly could have the organ played at their wedding or have their children baptised. This led to endless rows and he did once confess to me that he wished he had never made the regulations—but having done so, nothing would shift him.

The secret behind his retirement, and indeed his early death, was I am sure because he hated the changes in the world, and particularly in the Church, so much that he just opted out. Whenever we met in later years he would lecture me on the shortcomings of the Church with all his old vehemence and as if I were personally responsible.

I fear I have made him appear a rather unattractive figure and this is the side of him which many people saw and disliked. Yet he was a very affectionate and loyal friend while as a priest he took great care of his people, but like his friends, they had to toe the party line.

He was one of the most amusing and interesting companions I have ever known and I remember with enormous nostalgia the war-time expeditions we made, limited by shortage of petrol, looking at churches and houses in the vicinity of Oxford. He always knew about everything worth seeing and still whenever I visit a church and find something remarkable my immediate reaction is: 'I wonder if Alex knew about this?' and there is the nostalgic realisation that he is no longer there to ask.

Once we went on holiday together to Cornwall and visited every church on that haunted peninsular which now, for me, is far more haunted by Alex than by any of its prehistoric ghosts.

He had an amazing collection of postcards and could usually refute one by producing pictorial evidence of what he claimed. There is no doubt at that time he formed my tastes in many directions and I wish I had kept some of his letters written in an elegant hand and full of amusing gossip and comment.

A short while ago I had a sudden impulse to visit his grave which I found in a very unkempt cemetery where he lies surrounded by people whose names I recognised from those letters of his describing the monumental battles he had fought with them. It was a sad pilgrimage and there will always remain a lot of Alex I could never understand, and I knew him as well as anyone in the world.

He was at hand when I was ordained priest and had a good deal to do with the arrangement of my First Mass, which probably made it more exotic than it would otherwise have been. (During the war I met a chaplain who assured me he had witnessed in St. Paul's, Oxford, the marriage of a young man to the Church. This was Alex's First Mass, when he had carried a bouquet!)

Kenneth Kirk had recovered from his illness of the year before and the ordination was very splendid. Kirk was an impressive figure and performed ceremonies correctly with a slight air of boredom which made him appear much like a Roman prelate. The majority of Anglican bishops were always so anxious about ceremonies and handled holy water and incense—if they could be persuaded to do so—as if they would 'kick back'. I am a little embarrassed to confess that I swore my ordination oaths on the Roman Breviary. Since Alex had persuaded me to use it I carried it about with me as, in order to get the office completed, I had to make use of every odd moment. When the Registrar distributed New Testaments for the taking of the oaths he passed me by saying: 'I see you have one.' In any case one was only required to 'assent' to the 39 Articles. Canon (Nippy) Williams, who took the ordination retreat, is supposed to have said: 'I assent to the 39 Articles as I assent to the Oxford Gas Works. I am aware of their existence, I am at the present moment engaged in no active plan for their destruction, but it does not mean that I approve of them'.

I said my First Mass, with great awe, early in the morning of the following day. The high altar had been decorated by the Sisters with Madonna lilies, I was wearing a lace alb with red chasuble, which glittered like a beetle's skin, and had been loaned by Alex. The organ was played without cessation by a brilliant organist, Bobby Meade, a Frenchman who had been ordained into the Church of England although he never displayed any particular affection for Anglicanism and was what we called 'a Breviary-Boy'. As a final touch I had hired a professional tenor who sang at the offertory and during the Communion. There was a large congregation to whom I gave blessings and commemoration cards in the approved continental manner. I did not carry a bouquet but I had a rose on the altar which I gave to my mother.

The vicar was at my side and if I had done some of the things now required by the Sacred Congregation of Rites I think he would have struck me to the ground. Billy Favell was the server and he was the only person there who was able to come to the Silver Jubilee of the event.

I was much more use in the parish when I became a priest and there was plenty to do, the war making everything far more complicated. Funerals, from a parish that size, came with horrid regularity and the local florist rubbing her hands said to me: 'Very nippy today, keeps us very busy and I expect it does you too, Father!'

I shall never forget the funeral of an old man whose death bed I had attended. As the coffin was being lowered into the grave a woman stepped forward to throw some flowers. Another approached from the other side and tried to prevent her, so she began to throw the flowers at her tormentor. Then all hell broke loose for the mourners divided into two parties on either side of the grave began hurling the wreaths at each other in a complete silence which made their violence more sinister. It was the result of some bitter dispute over the will and it was reported to me many years later that one of the parties had said: 'I shall never forget how wonderful Fr. Stephenson was.'

I can only say that I am glad I have gone down to history in this role, for I had a headache and simply stood turning my head from side to side like a spectator at Wimbledon. At one point I said: 'This is a disgraceful scene', but at that moment a cross of lilies came straight at my head and I had to duck swiftly to avoid it, which rather destroyed the force of my rebuke. It was not until the undertakers, who had retired behind the hearse to have a smoke, came back and drove the contending parties out of range that I was able to complete the Burial Service.

I very much enjoyed parish work because I am fortunate enough to like people. When I used to stay in the Hospice at Walsingham I was fascinated by the high church ladies and used to think how wonderful it would be to minister to those of such elevated churchmanship. I had been much taken by one of them, a lady who lived in Sussex, but later moved to Walsingham after a bitter altercation with her vicar who had removed from the head of Our Lady a silver crown she had given.

It was she who made me join the Society of Mary and I was fascinated by her house which had a large image with a blue lamp in the hall and shrines of various saints in every other room, including the bathroom. She lived very comfortably and it was the mixture of sophistication and the exotic which I found irresistible. My mother who was not so impressed would refer rather acidly to: 'That commonplace lady you are so fond of', and set her face quite firmly against objects of piety at home except in our bedrooms.

Another experience in the same field was a lady who used to attend the poor little Church of the Annunciation, Brighton, although she lived rather grandly in Hove. I always called her

'Tante Annie' and for many years I thought her to be French as, I am sure, everyone else did so that I was very surprised to discover that she had merely stayed in France a good deal as a girl and adopted a French accent ever after. She managed to have a wonderful air of chic which gave complete authenticity to her pose.

She used to entertain all the vicars of Brighton's Anglo-Catholic churches to luncheon on Boxing Day and their curates on the day after to eat the scraps fallen from their masters' table. When I first appeared at the Annunciation she said of me: 'He will make the sort of young priest I like to have at my table.' I had my legs under it very often and the food was as good as a trip to Paris.

Cowley St. John had its full quota of devout women but they were of a more homely blend. Most of them worked in shops and got up to come to High Mass at 6 a.m. on days of obligation. The older ones had many of them been instructed by Fr. Benson himself, like the old lady who was the first person to whom I gave the Sacrament of Holy Unction. She was so frightened that I was going to miss anointing her feet that she thrust them out of the bed and died in the effort.

Another old lady of the same vintage calmly disobeyed everything the doctor told her saying firmly: 'Leave people alone and they live longer.'

I have never ceased to admire the single-minded devotion of the really converted high church woman. Some years ago there was a tragic motor smash near Walsingham when a priest was killed and his devout women passengers horribly injured. I went to see them in hospital where they were lying with almost everything broken except their necks, but their main worry was that they would have another vicar appointed who would not maintain the faith.

Some of the faithful at Cowley St. John were a little odd. There was an elderly nurse, who dressed like someone out of Dickens and who spent her whole day either in church or on errands of mercy. She really enjoyed collecting money for the church and was more than once picked up by the police for pestering people in the street. Then there was a formidable Irish lady, whose rich brogue made the recitation of the Litany of Our Lady a joy. She was distinctly peculiar as she kept all the lights and fires on in her house day and night saying that a nice young man from the Electricity Board had explained the new tariff and told her the more she used the cheaper it would be. Her memory got worse and worse and she would sometimes call at the vicarage to ask where she lived.

We had living in the parish a retired priest called Fr. de Waal who was a gentle and whimsical character. He always wore a frock coat and a top hat into which in summer he would put a dock leaf to keep himself cool. 'Party badge, my dear Father,' he would say of his clothes for when he was a young man Catholics had dressed in this way. When I was an undergraduate I had often seen him walking along the tow path and he was known by the rowing fraternity as 'the Bishop of Weirs Bridge'.

He was one of a generation who lived their whole life in the Church of England while behaving as though it didn't exist. His active ministry had been spent as a curate at Barnes where he and the vicar were life-long friends, but unfortunately did not have the same sort of religion. Fr. de Waal ran a separate show in the side chapel where he had Sung Mass and Vespers while Matins and Evensong were held in the main body of the church. I once asked him how he let people know about his services and he replied: 'Why, by postcard, of course.' He was a complete non-conformist for he had his own ideas about everything and no power on earth would make him change them, but he always managed to get his own way by a gentle mild persistence.

He hated all things Sarum but particularly Gothic vestments and if he went into a church where they were used he would produce a card of safety pins and turn them into the Latin shape as like as not ruining them completely. He used to go round saying Mass at different churches, but he would take a small bell which he could hold between his fingers and ring as he elevated the Host if there was no server, and a book which had 'Cash' on the front, but which he called 'My Missal' and had written himself. As he never said anything but a Votive Mass of St. Joseph, except on the very greatest feasts, there had not been much to write.

'I can't think why people will try to join in when one is saying Mass', he would remark plaintively, 'if they try it with me I go first fast and then slow and they don't keep it up.' He would always arrange to say Mass at the opposite side of Oxford from where he happened to be living and one would see him at a bus stop looking the other way when a bus came and so missing it. He would complain: 'I assure you, my dear Father, the Oxford buses never stop for me.'

He came twice a week and said a late Mass at SS. Mary & John where he was discovered by one of the Sisters dragging a clean alb around the sacristy floor. When he saw he was observed he said guiltily: 'Oh dear, I do so hate clean linen!'

It was not always easy to find a server for him at the hour he liked to say Mass and so he would walk down the road stopping people, raising his top hat and saying: 'Excuse me, madam, but can you answer Mass? I don't care what your religion is, but can you answer Mass?'

He liked to be asked to preach but one never quite knew what vintage the sermon would be and he surprised us one evening in 1940 by saying: 'Now that the dear boys are coming back from Ladysmith.' I was not surprised when he confided to me: 'I can't think why some people say they will only preach a sermon once, why I've preached some of mine hundreds of times.' I always enjoyed his illustrations and recall him once saying: 'Nature is a wonderful thing. Why I have seen whole paving stones tossed in the air by the common mushroom at Ealing.'

He had started a ward of the Confraternity of the Blessed Sacrament at Barnes which consisted of some old ladies who made vestments for poor parishes, but Fr. de Waal would only let them supply a chasuble and maniple, for he would say: 'God bless my soul, everyone's got a stole, burse and veil.' I once asked him what happened if someone insisted on having Gothic vestments and he replied: 'I simply tell them to make a Latin set and put a tail on it.' After he had come to live in Oxford he would ask local vicars if he could have Vespers in their church for his ward of C.B.S. When they asked how many he expected he would reply: 'God bless my soul, they won't be there, they all live in Barnes.'

Every year he would arrange a Sunday School treat and present it to a poor parish. They always had to start from the same place, even if it meant going back through the station from which they had set out, and he always took them to the same spot in the country. Unfortunately it was sold for building development and every year there was less and less country, until at last he was taking the children into the middle of a housing estate and the residents complained.

I asked him to be my confessor and I found him very comforting as he always went through my sins and made an excuse for each one. Should I confess to having murdered my aunt he would say: 'Of course aunts are notoriously tiresome, I can't think why more of them don't get themselves killed, in fact it can hardly be counted as a sin at all.' If he could think of no other excuse he would put it down to the daylight saving, which he hated, saying: 'With these ridiculous times and absurd arrangements one can't be surprised at any fall from grace.'

During his last illness I went to see him in bed and with some hesitation asked if he felt well enough to hear my confession. He at once took a purple stole from under the pillow and put it on. When we had finished he said contentedly: 'God bless my soul, I have enjoyed that.'

Some of the Cowley Fathers came to sing at his funeral and used the Proper for a Requiem from the Sarum Missal. I quite expected to hear a rap of protest from inside the coffin.

Cowley St. John was a wonderful parish in which to serve my title as it was a completely parochial church and almost all the large congregation lived in the parish and did not, as in so many so-called 'Anglo-Catholic centres' come from far and wide because they liked the particular brand of religion.

It was splendid to have a vicar who was always saying: 'Mirror, mirror on the wall, Who is the highest of us all' and determined that it should not be one of his curates. I remember what a blow I thought I had struck for the faith when I persuaded him to have the Prayers after Mass—now I have almost forgotten what they were!

I was wonderfully happy as I rode about the east Oxford streets on my blue bicycle finding them full of rich characters who endeared themselves to me, and I think that I endeared myself to them. Never for a moment did I regret my decision to become a priest. I was 'Father', in spite of my youth, greeted as such by the children, addressed so by those old enough to be mine and who had been taught a reverence for the office of a priest which made me feel that I must never do anything which would tarnish this image. I worked hard, but also played hard as I still had a lot of friends the other side of Magdalen Bridge.

Of course the financial help my parents gave me made it

possible for me to avoid any of the material hardships a curacy at that time was apt to impose. They gave me to the Church, as they paid for my training and supported me in my early years, so that I hope any good I may have done will be placed to their credit.

Happy as I was, there was a war on; all the time young men from the parish were being called up. A number of my personal friends were already in the forces, which was very upsetting for anyone of my age. I have never wanted to leave any job I have been doing nor any place where I have put down roots and God has always had to take me by the scruff of the neck to move me. In this case I simply cannot remember how the idea developed in my mind, for it suddenly came on me. It was like Pope John's explanation of how the Vatican Council came about. I simply woke up one morning and said to myself : 'I'm going to join the Navy.'

7
The Navy

I WENT TO SEE the Chaplain of the Fleet by appointment and was kept waiting in a small cloakroom outside his office. I sat demurely saying my Breviary while every now and then a very pretty Wren came to powder her nose. I wondered if I was being given a preliminary test to see if I was safe with Wrens and I kept my eyes strictly lowered on my book.

I certainly passed the test and was told to report to Portsmouth Barracks, for chaplains were what in the Navy are called 'makee learn'—those who are taught their job while doing it. So to Portsmouth I went after the agony of packing up in Oxford and was launched into a new life as if a fairy had waved a wand. Gone were my beaver hat and smart soutane and very soon my Breviary was tucked away unused as I was saying Morning and Evening Prayer with my fellow chaplains and even had Alex's reproving eye been upon me there just wasn't time for all those Nocturns.

The office of Chaplain in the Navy is a rank in itself and is given great marks of outward respect. It was heady wine that the sentry at the barrack gates presented arms every time I passed and I felt like a member of the chorus who has been popped straight into a leading part.

I was often asked by sailors about my rank and I always replied : 'I am the same rank as anyone with whom I happen to be talking, and if I'm talking to the Captain, I'm an Admiral.'

However we 'makee-learns' were soon put in our place by the Senior Chaplain at the barracks. Harold Beardmore was a completely naval figure for he had served as a midshipman in the Great War and so he knew the Service inside out. In some ways he was very like the vicar I had just left except that brass hats rather than bishops were the victims of his strong arm tactics.

Many years later I stayed with him in Basutoland, where he was archdeacon, and he was treating the colonial set-up in Maseru as if it were a naval establishment—and it was a great success. As he took me punctiliously to sign the Resident Commissioner's book, I could not help remembering a similar journey when I first arrived in Portsmouth to sign the Admiral's Book.

I never saw the chapel of the barracks as it had been destroyed in the bombing before I arrived, but a hut had been erected right in the heart of things and there we had daily Mass and said the Office while life hummed around us. For Sunday worship the Church of St. Michael and All Angels was used. This had been in its day a famous Anglo-Catholic centre and Dom Bernard Clements was one of its vicars before he became a monk. It had been built with the idea that there would be a big housing development in that part of Portsmouth, instead of which the dockyard had swallowed up all the space and St. Michael's was left with almost no parish. The war had finished off its eclectic congregation and it ceased to be a parish church.

I found it a depressing building with its empty tabernacle and untended shrines, all relics of its vanished past. I once went there to say Mass and found the naval verger opening drawers in the sacristy. When he saw me he said in the confidential voice of a gentleman's gentleman: 'And what would you like to wear this morning, sir?' producing at random a red dalmatic.

Portsmouth and Southsea were in a terrible state from the bombing and two famous churches had been destroyed. St. Agatha's, Landport, where Fr. Dolling had fought his battles, was a heap of ruins and almost incredibly—for to me it seemed as far away as the dark ages—his successor, Fr. Coles, was still there conducting services in one of the ruined chapels. Someone who had been his curate told me that he would never give any idea of what he was to do on Sunday till late on Saturday evening. If asked earlier in the week he would say: 'Oh go and boil your head.' Then at about 10 p.m. on Saturday he would call up the stairs: 'Will you say Mass at eight and preach at eleven tomorrow, Father, please?'

The other ruin was St. Matthew's, Southsea which had been built by Fr. Bruce Cornford, who raised a lot of money for the building by walking round with a five pound note pinned to his cassock and conducting a perpetual raffle, which caused more scandal in those days than it would now. He never forgot that the bishop had made a terrible fuss about consecrating the building and told him, amongst other things, that he could have an altar with a stone top and wooden legs or a wooden top and stone legs, but *not* a stone altar. Now the church lay in ruins and Mass was said in the sacristy, with a cupboard for the Holy Table.

I was given warm hospitality and friendship here by Ted Roberts and his curates as it was not possible to say Mass every day at the barracks and I was billeted in a rather seedy hotel in Southsea. I often said Mass in the old sacristy, but most of the services had been moved to the next door parish and the church called SS. Matthew & Bartholomew.

The old R.C. Chaplain at the barracks who had been in the Service for years said to me one day: 'That church of yours in Southsea has an odd dedication', he then added meditatively 'I suppose it's not so odd really—they were both members of the same mess.'

There were a lot of naval establishments around Portsmouth for which the chaplains at the barracks were responsible and on Sundays I took services in some odd places. I remember saying Mass in the Stoker's School where the table for the altar had been rigged against a wall which had some of the most filthy pictures I have ever seen outside a public lavatory scribbled on it. It seemed a very curious reredos for the celebration of the Holy Mysteries, but I have no doubt that today the more 'with-it' clergy would regard it as a perfect way of bringing every-day life into religion rather than vice versa, which my old-fashioned generation thought the right way round.

The congregation all sat on forms holding their hats in their hands and looking as if they were waiting on a railway platform and taking no part in the service. I turned round with the Holy Sacrament and said 'Behold the Lamb of God' but no one showed any sign of moving so I lapsed into service language and said sharply 'Double up' to which they reacted immediately.

When I was first ordained I used to write out sermons in black exercise books which I have still got and which impress me very much when I dip into them today as I can no longer remember where I pinched the ideas from. Once I joined the Navy I discovered that the only recipe for preaching if one wanted to hold the attention of one's congregation was to 'stand up, speak up and shut up'. Since then I have seldom taken a manuscript into the pulpit with me. Of course I forget half the things I intend to say, but this is no bad thing!

A priest once said to me: 'I don't mind people looking at their watches while I'm preaching, but I do object to them shaking them to see if they've stopped.'

Harold Beardmore was fairly tough with us and would send us off to do things with little time to make any preparations. It was rather like being Fr. Coles' curate. I remember him telling me one morning to go and give a lecture in the cells there and then. I walked across the 'quarter deck'—the Navy uses the same terms ashore as at sea and I have seen a Petty Officer walking down the pavement shouting up at a building 'Darken ship'—and as I walked the short distance to the Detention Quarters I couldn't think of anything to lecture about. I was not made more comfortable by the sound of the Master at Arms opening the cell doors, and using a spate of foul language.

I was soon confronted by the most surly and resentful looking audience I have ever had to face. We looked at each other for a few moments and at last I said: 'This is much worse for me than it is for you.' After that we became friends and I talked to them about bull fighting, of which I knew almost nothing, but it held their attention.

I'm sure that most of 'the f-ing and b-ing which went on in the Navy was really from lack of vocabulary so that it padded out conversation. On the whole the sailors were very particular when the chaplain was around and anyone who swore was firmly thrown out of the mess.

Most of the bombing was over and Portsmouth, particularly around the dockyard, was in a terrible mess. There were constant Air Raid warnings and we all went scuttling into the shelters—which I found terribly claustrophobic. Once an alarm sounded during a church service I was conducting and as we made for the shelter I was crafty enough to seize an alms bag and took up a record collection.

On Sunday evenings there was a big variety show at the British Sailors Society and I often had to go along and give what was known as the Epilogue at the end of the performance. The artists were warned that they were to give no indication that the show was coming to an end or the audience would all get up and leave. One had to stand in the wings and dash in and start talking to one's 'captive congregation' before they had a chance of getting to their feet.

There can be no doubt that the Navy very soon ironed out the rather prissy clerical attitudes which I had picked up largely from Alex, with his very 'French Seminarian' ways of going on.

Everyone at the barracks was expecting a draft chit and this included the chaplains. H.M.S. *Penelope* was in the dockyard being refitted and we knew that one of us would be appointed as her chaplain, and I think we all hoped we might be the one chosen. It was in fact a death sentence for she later was torpedoed and sank with all hands, including the chaplain.

When my draft chit came it did not involve much of a move as I was appointed assistant chaplain to the Royal Marine Barracks, Eastney, which is at the east end of Portsea Island. I was bitterly disappointed. I had joined the Navy to go to sea and, although Harold Beardmore assured me it was a plum of a job which I had only been given on his special recommendation, it seemed to me a terrible anti-climax to be stranded ashore. I knew nothing about the Marines and had no wish to do so.

It did not take me long to learn that to serve with the Royal Marines in one of their own barracks was a rare experience and that I was indeed very lucky. Eastney is a fine barracks with an impressive frontage on the sea and before the war people had come from London on Sundays to witness the Church Parade, so magnificent was it considered to be in this setting.

The church was outside the back gate of the barracks, large, red brick and with very little charm. As there was a sentry on the gate who asked all ranks, except officers, where they were going there was little inducement for any Marine to use the church unless marched there behind a vast sixty-piece band. On arrival the band would replace their brass instruments with strings and the sound, if not the ceremonial, was very like Bart's, Brighton.

The chaplain was Jack Wilson, a large rather fearsome figure whose severe poker-face hid one of the most humorous and affectionate natures I have ever known. We took to each other at once and we had a lot of fun in what used to be known as 'advancing the churchmanship'. We started a daily Mass to which we persuaded some of the officer's wives to come. One morning two of the most senior came on the same day and each was obviously astounded to see the other. Jack came bouncing into the sacristy before I had got the vestments off my back and said: 'The Brigadier and Second Commandant are very sorry they couldn't be here but they are walking barefoot to the Shrine of St. Richard of Chichester.'

He was a master of quick repartee which he could deliver without batting an eyelid. When we went to robe for something at the Cathedral a bossy woman who was directing traffic said: 'Are you clergymen?'

'No,' replied this enormous figure, 'dancing girls', and pushed past her into the vestry.

He would say the most devastating things as asides to me when we were both in church together and the congregation, if they saw his lips move at all, would have thought from his face that he was making some pious comment. When we were saying the Office together he would end a lesson from Job by saying in a liturgical voice: 'And I am sure we are both very much the wiser.'

His sense of humour did not often desert him and when a bomb dropped in his garden I dashed along at once to find the house in a terrible mess. The first thing that Jack said on seeing me was: 'This is the first time I've come through this front door and not been told to wipe my feet.'

Our most successful innovation was to start a Sung Mass at 9.30 on Sundays. The excuse for this was that the bugler boys were forced to come to the Parade Service and sit in a corner where they could see nothing. The Brigadier thought it a good idea to have an earlier service to which they could come if they wished, which of course they did as it was much shorter and they did not have to use so much spit and polish.

This was the first time I had ever started anything like this from scratch and so many things went wrong on the first Sunday that I almost gave up in despair. The organist kept giving notes with such persistent regularity that I turned from the altar and shook my fist at him. However, little by little things smoothed out and I believe that the 9.30 Sung Eucharist still goes on at Eastney to this day.

The thing that worried us most was that hardly a man ever came to Communion on Sunday. The reason was not hard to discover for the barrack rooms were scrubbed out at that time and while those wanting to go to church could get permission to do so it is not hard to imagine what their fellows who were left scrubbing away said about it.

The barrack routine was as unchangeable as the laws of the Medes and Persians, so the only solution was to rig an altar in my office and have an early Mass before the cleaning began. Of course the real answer would have been to have an Evening Mass, but in those days we behaved as if it were better for people not to receive the Sacrament at all than sacrifice the sacred principles of Fasting Communion. Later when I was in a ship I would allow my empty stomach to suffer the greatest discomfort in a rough sea rather than put anything into it when I was saying a late Mass.

Every week there was an intake of newly enlisted men and those who said they were C. of E. were marched for an interview with me. I had never before realised how pagan England had become. When I asked if they had been baptised as like as not they would say that they had the mark on their left arm. Usually I could persuade one or two to be confirmed and would give them a crash course and get them to a bishop.

In this way I attended confirmations all over the town. Jack Wilson came with me once and the bishop preached about Samson. Jack said out of the side of his mouth: 'When I'm a bishop I'll come to your church and preach about Snow White and the Seven Darfs.'

One morning a Company Commander rang me up and asked if I knew anything about a religion called 'Anglo-Catholic' as he had got a boy with this stamped on his identity disc and he was refusing to go on Church Parade. I said: 'Send him over to me and I will persuade him that he's C. of E.' When he arrived looking sheepish I said at once, 'I don't remember seeing you at Mass.' The answer to the mystery of his disc was that he had been employed in making them and had stamped his own. I phoned back his Company Commander and said that I had convinced him that he was C. of E. and would he have him woken early so that he could come to early church next Sunday.

I enjoyed the life of the mess and the friendship of the residents in 'Tea Pot Row' as we called the Senior Officers' houses. Some of the ladies did not live in as great a degree of mutual charity as could have been wished. During the decoration of the church at Christmas we heard an icy voice say: 'That is my piece of holly you have deliberately taken', and Jack and I fled and locked ourselves cravenly in the vestry as he said: 'I can face the bombing, but not this.'

I was constantly urging Jack to get me sent to sea, not because I was unhappy but people went out from the barracks and returned having done all sorts of exciting things and I felt that I had just sat on my bottom in an office and said grace at the weekly guest night which was carried out with full ceremonial, the table loaded with trophies and the vast band playing away in the gallery.

At last marching orders came for both of us. I was to report to Glasgow to be chaplain of a new cruiser and Jack was to go to the top of the list as Chaplain of the Fleet where he needed every ounce of humour in him to keep him sane.

The mess gave me a farewell party and removed my trousers afterwards, which is the highest sign of affection in those circles. Jack's last words of wisdom to me were: 'Remember when you get in a ship "Softee softee catchee monkey", and then you'll be able to do anything you like.'

8

At Sea

A SPECIAL TRAIN WENT NIGHTLY to Scotland divided, like ancient Gaul, into three parts: one for the Army, one for the Navy, and one for the Air Force. A sleeper had been booked for me in the naval part but there was such confusion at Euston that I was pushed into a seat in the Air Force section of the train.

I was feeling rather miffed about this but, when I saw an Admiral walking up and down the corridor trying to find somewhere even to sit down, I didn't feel quite so deprived and under-privileged. I sat up the whole night reading *The Song of Bernadette* which had just been published and was a farewell present from friends at Eastney.

Glasgow was anything but inviting when we arrived at 6 a.m. as a thin drizzle was falling. I at once went to Naval Headquarters and presented my draft chit which had a code on it as, for security reasons, I was not supposed to know the name of the ship I was joining. In fact I knew very well that it was H.M.S. *Ceylon,* for one of the doctors from Eastney had gone to join her a couple of weeks earlier.

The night staff were still on duty and the Senior Officer said: 'Why not go to the Club, old boy, and have a bath and some breakfast. Toddle back here about nine and they'll fix you up with some transport.' I failed to find the Officers' Club but I did discover the R.C. cathedral where a lot of old Irish women, with shawls over their heads and faces like saints were singing a hymn which began: 'Mungo, by thy sweet name our children we will call.' I was told later that the things they really

111

call their children when out of church would make a sailor blush.

Sharp at nine I was back at Naval Headquarters and the day staff had come on duty. They passed my chit from hand to hand and one of them whistled. There was a muttered conference and then the senior said: 'I'm sorry Padre, but I'm afraid she's sailed, but you just go off to the Club and we'll make some enquiries.' I was not going to fall for that one again and so I insisted on remaining till something was settled. After a lot of telephone calls, which they made so security-minded that the person on the other end didn't know what they were trying to find out, they were forced to say the name of the ship, and discovered that she was heading for the Isle of Arran.

So I went by train to some small west coast harbour where I went aboard a drifter and at last caught up with the *Ceylon* at Lamlash, which was an attractive anchorage with the mountainous island in the background.

A smart new motor boat was sent over to collect me and I was somewhat nonplussed to find not only the Captain and Commander but the entire wardroom assembled on the quarter deck to greet me. I was the last member of the crew to join and they had been expecting me for some days so that speculation as to what the Chaplain would be like had risen to fever pitch and they all turned out to see the worst for themselves.

My cabin was a large one off the Marine Mess Deck and I soon had a sign reading 'The Vicarage' on the door. Once we got to the tropics it would have been more accurate to have had 'Hades' on it, for it was unbearably hot, and I spent as little time there as possible.

Unfortunately on my first night in a bunk I went to sleep with the forced draught playing directly on me and when I woke in the morning my neck was completely fixed to one side. It was not easy to be jolly and natural with people I had only just met with my head turned on my shoulder.

The two most important people in any ship are the Captain and the Commander and I was not long in discovering that we had a rum selection. The Captain was a good-looking man and an intelligent, efficient naval officer, but he had had a difficult relationship with his mother which had completely warped his character. She had made it abundantly clear that she preferred her other son and always denigrated any success he ever had. This had given him a positive fear and dislike of women and

112

had made him resent the happiness and success of other people. The Commander was a small, wiry, rather monkey-like man of enormous vitality and almost incredible inefficiency. He was a terrific showman and one began by wondering if he was the most remarkable man one had ever met, or the biggest liar on earth.

He was a complete Baron Münchausen, but in all his tall stories he had got enough of the true facts to make it difficult to sort out the fictional elements. He had several roles he delighted to play—the naval hero, who in command of a destroyer had been almost completely responsible for the evacuation of Dunkirk; the great inventor who had produced the idea behind most of the scientific achievements since the beginning of the war; the champion amateur jockey and polo player, whose exploits had become a legend. He had a puckish charm which completely disarmed one's critical faculties. But it would have been hard to find anyone more insensitive to his charm and hypercritical of his inefficiency than the Captain.

I soon found myself a 'buffer state' between the two of them and was witness of some fantastic scenes. There is a very historic photograph of them both at the Commissioning Ceremony for they are both smiling, and I think it is doubtful if they ever smiled again in each other's company for the three years they served together.

Given this situation it is remarkable that we had one of the happiest wardrooms in the Fleet and this was largely due to the Commander's wonderful social gifts. However junior the officer one had as a guest he would always come up and greet him warmly and remember him at once if he came again. He played up to any part expected of him. When a bishop came aboard he said in an emotional voice: 'Our chapel is only a little place amidships, but the life of the whole ship revolves around it.' The bishop said to me afterwards: 'You are lucky having a Commander who is such a keen churchman,' and I had to confess that I had never even seen him in the chapel.

It was the provision of this chapel which was one of my first tasks when I joined the ship as no space for this purpose had been set aside in the design. In fact there wasn't even a chalice, for a petty officer was in cells on a charge of having sold stores ashore but as he had destroyed the supply notes no one really knew what he had pinched, but it was strongly suspected that he had pawned the chalice. It was suggested that I should visit him in cells and ask if he wanted Holy Communion to see if he blushed!

I had all my own gear and so I began at once saying Mass in my cabin on weekdays and in the recreation space on Sundays. I was lucky enough from the beginning to find one or two people prepared to serve Mass, including a Chief Petty Officer who had been brought up at the Annunciation, Brighton.

I was determined to have a proper chapel and began by getting permission to use the Admiral's sea cabin—this was vacant as, although fitted for it, we were not at the moment carrying an admiral. It was long and narrow and almost passage-like in shape but it could hold about six people and I began having Mass and Evening Prayers there.

A terrific fight for space was going on between the heads of most departments in the ship. The struggle centred round the two empty hangars amidships, for we were designed to carry aircraft but by this time in the war they had ceased to be used from cruisers and so all this lovely space was due for reallotment. The Commander always agreed with the last person who had been talking to him so that all the heads of departments were quite sure they were going to have a big slice and it soon became obvious that there would be a lot of disappointments. I strongly suspected that, if I were not very careful, the space for a chapel would remain a pious hope.

My trump card was that I was already in the Admiral's sea cabin and I made it quite clear that I wouldn't move out till there was a proper chapel. In the final share out I got a better deal than I expected and the chapel was big enough to hold thirty or forty people. This was much better than in many ships where it was often little more than a cupboard deep in the bowels of the vessel. One chaplain I knew always said Mass in Latin for the engines made such a noise that he claimed no one could hear a word he was saying in any case.

This struggle had been taking place during our working-up period which we did at Scapa Flow. While we were there George VI came on a visit to the Home Fleet and all the chaplains were required to leave their own flocks and provide a living reredos in the cinema on the Isle of Flotta where the monarch was to worship God.

We all sat up in rows wearing scarf and hood, and I had on

a rather *outré* version of an Oxford M.A. hood which had been designed by Alex Lawson to look as much like a Roman mozetta as possible with scarlet buttons down the front. After the service the whole proceedings were held up as the King asked to see me and wanted to know what my hood was as he said he couldn't take his eyes off it during the service. All round admirals were pawing the ground with impatience as I tried to explain that when men wore wigs in the 18th Century the hole had to be made big enough to go over their heads. The King listened intently : 'But all those buttons down the front?' he asked.

'Those', I was forced to admit, 'are a bit of nonsense of my own.' He laughed and moved on with the carefully timed programme to which this interlude had been an unexpected interruption. My Captain told me that after this several people had said to him : 'I hear you've got a cardinal as chaplain in your ship.' He was rather pleased.

It was when we went to Devonport for a final refit before going into active service that I managed to get the chapel fitted out. This was the first chapel I had had the chance of constructing myself since my amateur attempts in the loft over the stables at Henfield and I determined that it should leave no one in any doubt of the churchmanship. Most of the fittings were made by the tradesmen in the ship. The altar which had a proper altar stone procured for me by Bertha Travers of Pax House (an excellent Anglo-Catholic repository which she brought to birth and then ran into the ground through her strong-mindedness and lack of business acumen), was made as a cupboard to hold frontals and other gear. The credence table by its side was also a vestment chest with drawers.

Of course there was a large tabernacle and four candles on the gradine. As a shrine of Our Lady I had a picture of Our Lady of Perpetual Succour which, when we had Goanese cooks and stewards, excited them to so great a fervour that they bought candles ashore to burn in front of it. The North Country boy who cleaned the chapel did not appreciate this and would say in his flat Manchester accent : 'Those bloody niggers have been making a mess again.'

When it was finished I looked upon it like Almighty God and thought it was very good.

Some splendid women, who were members of the Church Union in Devon, had a guild making things for naval chaplains and they provided me with frontals, tabernacle veils and linen of all sorts.

After the war, when the *Ceylon* was in action again in Korean waters, I had a letter from a chaplain who had just joined; he said it was the best equipped chapel he had found in the Service and as he had gathered I was responsible he wanted me to know that the things were still there in use.

It was a great frustration that when we first got to sea we almost at once picked up some survivors who had to be billeted in the chapel and so I had to empty the tabernacle and say Mass again in my cabin until we dropped them at Gibraltar.

We had slipped out of Plymouth Sound under cover of darkness and, in spite of strict security, we all knew that we were bound for the Far East. I had had embarkation leave which I spent with my parents at Henfield and my father had walked with me to the railway station when I left. It was the last time I saw him, for unknown to any of us he was already suffering from cancer which killed him twelve months later.

So we forged our way through the Mediterranean at the time of the Sicily landings when it was bubbling with activity like a witch's cauldron.

It is no part of this chronicle to tell of our war record but the following is so strange that it may well have a place. The doctors, the dentist and myself used to lend a hand with the cyphering. It was not official and not very pleasant, as it had to be done in a stuffy hole where the cypher books were kept. Most of it was figures and chart readings and meant nothing to the layman, but we were assured that anything doubtful would be queried at once from the bridge.

One day when I was deciphering the Situation Report I got a figure wrong. The curious thing is that it was the only figure, other than the right one, in the thousands of permutations, which made any sense. It was thought by the navigator to be rather an odd course but the landings had confused the usual pattern of shipping. Next day we were several hundred miles out of station having sailed blithely through mine fields and all manner of hazards. The curious thing was that we were the only ship to sail through the Mediterranean at that time without seeing either a plane or a submarine; and another ship, which followed the course we should have taken a few hours later, was torpedoed and sunk. You can make what you like of it!

The Captain said: 'I don't know whether to recommend you for a Court Martial or a medal.' The positive benefit was that the voluntary boys were never asked to help again with the cyphering.

When we got to the Red Sea it began to get hot and on Sunday I put on a cotta instead of a surplice which I thought would be cooler. The Captain remarked as we were walking up to church: 'That's a curious garment you're wearing.' So I simply said: 'It's tropical rig', to which he replied: 'What a good idea, I've never seen one before, but it's very sensible.' So after that I took to wearing a cotta on all occasions little thinking I should live to see the point of Fr. Hack's contemptuous name of 'bum freezer' for that particular garment.

I found that being chaplain in a ship was like being vicar of a very nice small, compact parish. The sense of community was a reality for we all depended on each other to keep the ship afloat, and if it sank we all sank together. It is extraordinary how adversity binds human beings together, and it was very noticeable after we had been in danger that everyone was much nicer and more tolerant. Of course we got on each other's nerves a bit in so confined a space and, having lived in a ship, I shall never believe that it is only women who enjoy gossip and making trouble.

I found the truth of what Jack Wilson had taught me, that if one waited till one's mess-mates knew and trusted one, it was possible to do what one liked in the chapel without opposition. The number who came to Mass was never very large, but I suppose in proportion to the ship's company of about a thousand souls it was much the same as an average parish of that size would have been. When it came to Holy Week I was able to have some form of the ceremonies of the last three days and organise a watch before the Blessed Sacrament; also from time to time I gave Benediction to the small inner group of really keen communicants. Once very boldly at Corpus Christi I gathered sympathetic chaplains and their flocks from other ships for Vespers of the Blessed Sacrament and Benediction. I felt that H.M.S. *Ceylon* ought to appear in the Navy List, like those guest houses advertising in the *Church Times*, as 'near church with full Catholic privileges'.

One or two of the officers were sympathetic and regular communicants. It was a great example that the Gunnery Officer,

117

usually the toughest nut in any ship, always came to Mass every Sunday even if he had been on the morning watch. The Paymaster-Commander was an old-fashioned churchman who raised his eyebrows slightly at some of the goings-on, but he was a great man for gadgets and he took an interest in making the Christmas Crib and created something which would have been a credit to an Italian church. We always imagined that if the ship sank we should discover that Pay had invented all sorts of things to make life comfortable in the water and would have a floating book rest with self-turning pages such as he used at breakfast.

The Captain confided in me that he did not come to Communion much because he could not bear drinking out of the chalice after other people. I explained to him that it was perfectly possible to receive the sacrament in one kind. He thought this was a terribly good idea and adopted the practice, much to the surprise of the more knowing who thought that I must have converted him to very extreme views—which was far from the truth.

Life at sea fell into a very pleasant rhythm. The ship's company gathered on the quarter-deck for Divisions at which there were Prayers—I believe the Navy is the only one of the Services to start the day with an official act of worship. I managed to have Mass every morning in the chapel and always got someone to serve so that I was sure of a congregation.

Most other people in the ship were watch-keeping but in the dog watches I would go and sit on the fo'c'sle where the ordinary seamen—who were neither on watch nor sleeping— would come and chat if they wished. It was at these moments one felt the advantage of not having rank in the accepted sense. It is very easy in the Navy to be regarded as an 'officer's chaplain', but on the other hand if he spends too much time in the Mess Decks the chaplain is resented, because the men, quite unnecessarily, feel that it places too great a strain on their good behaviour.

When we went to action stations the chaplain had no particular job, but I used to wander around between the bridge and below decks to tell those on damage control duty what was happening aloft, as it is the waiting for something to happen which is the greatest strain. We were lucky in never suffering a direct hit, but the difference in being bombed on land and at sea is that in the former case one seldom knows what the plane is aiming at—a ship knows only too well!

There was a lot of time at sea for reading and talking—sometimes in the dark on the quarter deck people would open their hearts and tell me what was really worrying them which in daylight and other circumstances they would have found too embarrassing. I have heard many confessions leaning over the rail watching the phosphorescent wake of the ship stream behind us like a white carpet.

The memories of those years come crowding in on me such as our arrival in Bombay on the Feast of St. Francis Xavier, and visiting the Cowley Fathers who still held the missionary torch on a small island of charity in the midst of a sea of indescribable poverty. I can never get out of my mind the scenes I later witnessed in Calcutta during the Bengal famine. I saw then an India with its pukka sahibs' clubs which has now been swept away but so many of its human problems still remain although the British are no longer at hand to blame for them.

The Eastern Fleet was based on the lovely island of Ceylon after which our ship was named so that when people said: 'This is the Chaplain of Ceylon' on introducing me, there was an astonished pause and then as like as not they asked: 'What particular part of Ceylon?' I have so many memories of that island; of Douglas Horsley, the Bishop of Columbo, with dancers from Kandy going in front of him as they went in procession for a confirmation up amongst the Tea Estates; of the enormous harbour of Trincomalee where the Eastern Fleet was based and where we spent much of our time complaining about it being a 'hole in the jungle'—which of course it was.

I remember too going ashore on Christmas Eve with the Midshipmen to cut great branches of flowers out of the jungle. The chapel looked marvellous but by the time of the Midnight Mass the flowers had all died and stank like corpses while horrifying, nightmarish insects crept out and danced before me on the altar.

A crazy old Admiral, who flew his flag in our ship and insisted on being put ashore every afternoon with someone detailed as a companion to walk with him is another vivid memory. He just forged his way through the jungle regardless of obstacles and when I went with him we came to a cliff and he went over the edge hanging on the creepers like Tarzan shouting to me to follow him.

Then there were the long journeys we made: down to South Africa, far east to Australia striking at targets in Sumatra and Malaya and, when the Japanese were on the run, coming up to Rangoon and finding the city completely sacked, the cathedral have been used as a saki distillery and what had been the 'high church' as a brothel—it was dedicated to the Holy Innocents!

So many more memories of people than places. Wonderful periods of leave with a family in South Africa at a farm near Pietermaritzburg; and with an Australian doctor and his wife, where a whole village took half the ship's company at a time and made us forget the thousands of miles we were from home.

One evening I was having dinner with some wealthy Ceylonese who had a wonderful collection of ivories and they asked me where in England they could offer an exquisite baroque image of Our Lady carved out of a single tusk of ivory. In what must have been a moment of inspiration I thought of the empty niche at Canterbury Cathedral which had once held the image of Our Lady Undercroft. And there it is today making me feel that the small part I played in getting it there may counterbalance some of my heavy misdeeds.

The sight of 'The Lady in White' at Durban singing away at the end of a breakwater, as she did to every ship that came and went is yet another memory, and then getting to know her as an intimate friend. In her memoirs she describes me as 'the handsomest man I had ever seen'! I leave the book around my guest room with a marker in it!!

What I felt was the epitome of Durban hospitality was that when we arrived I had news that my father had died, but life had to go on so I went ashore and saw the head of the South African Women's Auxiliary Services to fix up leave and entertainments for the troops. She said that if officers wanted dates she would like to see them first, as she always knew the right girl. Just to prove it she wanted to make a date for me that evening. I tried to refuse politely, but when she got very pressing I was forced to tell her that I had just had news of my father's death. She said at once: 'I know exactly the girl—her father died last week.'

Memories of all the many churches in which I ministered: of St. John the Divine, Durban, where I had a Requiem sung for my father as they had a choir school, and of old Fr. Fairbourne, who had built the church, having returned from England in the 1920s determined to recreate what he had seen at the first Anglo-Catholic Congress; of St. Paul's, Colombo, looking like a flower garden at High Mass on Easter Day with all the colourful saris the women were dressed in. (The Singhalese vicar had once tried his vocation at Cowley and been expelled from the novitiate for locking Fr. Longridge in the lavatory which was regarded as a sign that he had no vocation.)

There was a time when we seemed to have been away from home for so long that it was hard to remember what England was like and we had the disturbing news of buzz bombs which was a worry to those of us with families in the south of England. V.E. Day came and went but we still soldiered on against the Japanese. We had a service of thanksgiving when we heard of peace in Europe. I put on a scarf and hood and when the Captain saw me he said: 'If I'd known you were going to dress up like that, Padre, I'd have put on my Aggie Weston blue ribbon.' (Agnes Weston was the great Apostle of Temperance in the Navy.)

The Captain began the service with a little speech in which he said: 'Now we are very thankful today to many people and I will mention them in order of seniority, first Almighty God'! Second was Winston Churchill, but I was thankful God came first!

The tropics began to take its toll of my energy. The first hot season I often borrowed a bicycle when we were at Trinco and went cycling along the jungle tracks. The second year I spent most spare time on the beach and the third mostly lying under an awning on the quarterdeck itching all over with prickly heat.

One afternoon which seemed like any other I joined some friends who were going to bathe but felt I must also go and see one of the seamen who was sick, so after I had been in the water I dressed and said to my companions: 'I'll meet you at the jetty as I'm going to the hospital.' These were the truest words I have ever spoken for, taking a short cut through the jungle, I fell over thirty feet down a disused well, breaking both my legs with such complications that it was almost three years before I got out of the various hospitals into which I landed myself.

9

In Hospital

ALL MY LIFE I had had a dream of falling. I floated down and down and then before I reached the bottom awoke in terror. Since I fell down the well in Trinco I have never had that dream again and I can only conclude that my subconscious no longer has the nerve to fool me with a sensation which I now know was entirely phoney.

When I fell I certainly didn't float and arrived at the bottom before I had much idea what was happening. Someone once worked out from my weight and the distance I fell the speed at which I must have been moving when I hit the jagged rock at the bottom and I could quite understand why the journey hadn't taken long. Many people have since asked me: 'How could you possibly fall down a well?', and I can only reply that it is remarkably easy to do if you don't know that it's there. I was looking at a lizard running up a tree, followed it round the other side and down I went.

Both my legs broke on impact with the rock, for there was only a little brackish water at the bottom. I have been told that if they had not done so my spine would have taken the full shock with more serious consequences.

The first thing of which I was conscious was a terrible pain in my right foot as if it were being gnashed by teeth. A few weeks before I had been crossing a rope bridge where some crocodiles were lying in the mud below as if waiting for some-one to fall off. I felt a sudden rage against them, picked a stone from the bank and threw it with an unwonted accurate aim hitting one of them in the middle of the head. All that happened was that the creature opened one sinister eye and fixed it on me as if to say: 'I shall remember that.' When I felt teeth in my foot I saw that eye quite clearly in my imagination and for one terrible moment I thought: 'Oh God, he's got me.' I was so relieved when I found I was alone in the well that all other horrors paled.

I have never discovered how long I was down there—it seemed like eternity and I can remember invoking the help of Our Lady of Walsingham. At last black faces appeared over the side strongly outlined against the blue of the sky and then went away. Then someone spoke to me in English and I tried to answer with the stiff upper lip, which we are taught at school is the proper way to face adversity, as if falling down a well were an everyday pastime. There was another long wait and I tried to pray, but could find little more to say than 'Lord have mercy', which is a good prayer for all seasons.

A doctor was found on the beach and a rope procured from somewhere and he was let down. If only I had been able to faint at this moment I could have been hauled out like a sack of potatoes, but I never seem able to lose consciousness unless slugged really hard. The doctor discovered that my left leg was broken and made a rough splint tearing up his own shirt to tie it on. He then asked if I could take any weight on my right foot and I replied: 'I can do anything to get out of this bloody place.'

Thus I was hauled up on my broken foot and when I got to the top it was almost at right angles to my leg. There was a dreadful moment when they nearly dropped me down again, but lots of black hands grabbed at me and pulled me over the side.

An ambulance was brought as close as possible and I was carried on an improvised stretcher over very uneven ground, but they had brought no morphia and so was I jogged along with my bones grinding at every jolt. As everyone was dispersing pathetic shouts were heard in the distance—they had left the doctor down the well!

The hospital at Trinco was fairly primitive and being run partly by the Army and partly by the Navy. It was a Wren doctor on duty and she tried to make bright conversation. When I taxed her about this later she said that her only thought had been to get some dope into me as swiftly as possible so she was not attending to what she was saying and was surprised, in the circumstances, that I should remember.

Once she had given me a shot I lapsed into the blissful unconsciousness into which I had been longing to escape from the nightmare of pain. I have since been told that the doctors considered removing my right leg then and there regarding it as a 'write off', but decided that the shock might be too much for me—and they were probably right.

When I became conscious I was done up in plaster, but in the first few days I was taken off several times to the operating theatre although I had no idea what was being done to me. I now know that the plasters would not set in the damp heat (the naval doctors were quite certain it was because they were sub-standard army medical supplies) and so the pins they had put into my fracture all fell out.

Pain is a strange thing and isolates one from one's fellows and I could understand animals who go away and curl up in a corner to suffer alone. I have only the haziest memory of those days of pain and weakness, but I can remember saying to the chaplain: 'Am I going to die?' and his replying: 'They seem to think there is a chance of it at the moment. Do you want the Sacraments?' Until that moment I had not fully realised how ill I was, but I was in such pain and discomfort that the thought of death, holding a welcome promise of relief, was not alarming. I gasped out some sort of confession and was anointed. I was heavily doped and as I shut my eyes and drifted into unconsciousness I thought: 'This is it', and tried to commend my soul to the mercy of God. When I next became fully conscious I realised that I was still in the ward and knew that I was not going to die.

I had never been a patient in hospital before and I was deeply moved by the intuition of the night sister when I was very ill. She moistened my mouth and eased my pillows just when I needed it most and was too weak to ask for help. The hospital chaplain was very attentive and brought me Holy Communion every day. When I was a bit better he visited and talked to me a lot. He was due to go home and I was astonished to learn that on leaving the hospital he immediately made his submission to the Church of Rome. I was surprised that he had never said a word to me about this and have always admired his delicacy in resisting the temptation of unburdening himself upon a sick man when he must have been enduring considerable inner turmoil. He later returned to the Church of England and when I met him again referred to his period in a Roman Seminary by saying he considered it: 'As good a way as any of getting one's war neuroses out of one's system.'

By the time his replacement arrived I had been moved into a tiny room off one of the wards and had a spike through my left heel attached to weights and was being pumped with penicillin—then only recently discovered and enormously expensive. Unfortunately the bugs I had chummed up with down the well seemed to thrive on it and so the thousands of pounds it cost might just as well have been flushed down the closet.

The new chaplain had been a curate at St. Mary's, Graham Street, and a student at Chichester before my time so we had much in common.

The Matron of the Army part of the hospital was also a keen Anglo-Catholic and often came to see me, although I was not strictly in her territory. She would tell me of other members of the staff who were 'high' and say: 'She's one of us', in such a conspiratorial voice that I felt as if we shared a vice in common, but I have never forgotten her kindness.

The heat was a great burden and, although there was a punkah above the bed which kept the air moving, the electricity by which it worked would often fail. Then small flies would come and irritate around my eyes while I was too weak to brush them away. This weakness grew greater and greater so that I spent most of the day in a semi-conscious state although I was in more discomfort than pain. I was again put on the danger list and my anxious mother in England informed of this.

I am now amused that the doctors, having been unable to find any reason for my decline, came to the conclusion that I had given up the will to live. To try to stir some interest in me the Sister sent in one of the men from the ward to play chess with me. I was almost too weak to lift the pieces so she made him read a story from P. G. Wodehouse—he read abominably. The result has been that I cannot see a chess board without wincing and am about the only person in England who cannot raise a smile at the wit of Wodehouse.

At last the laboratory discovered that a somewhat rare malarial parasite was knocking my white corpuscles for six and I was given a series of blood transfusions at once—which worked like a miracle. I continued to get attacks of malaria for some years and I was able to distinguish it from flu because it always made me so self-pitying—a disease from which I do not normally suffer very much. Whenever I began to think that nobody loved me I knew I had malaria.

When I came off the danger list I was allowed to have visitors and saw many of my mess-mates. They told me that the Commander had excelled himself in drama on the evening of my accident. He made a broadcast to the ship's company and began in a voice charged with emotion : 'I have the most tragic news to impart to you', so that everyone who heard him thought we must have lost the war and was quite relieved when, after a dramatic pause, he continued : 'Our beloved chaplain has met with a terrible accident.'

The energetic old Admiral with whom I had gone walking in the jungle came to see me and thought I ought to be employed in some way so he brought me tools and a piece of wood and said he would come and see what sort of ship I had carved when he returned from Java, where he was going to receive the surrender of the Japs. I chipped away miserably and inefficiently while the sister was furious at the mess it all made. However things in Java did not prove as simple as the Admiral expected so I had left Trinco before he returned and with relief I threw the whole lot overboard, tools and all!

The war was now completely over and the hospital was flooded by casualties from the peace celebrations, the sounds of which I had heard from my bed. At the same time my messmates came with news that orders had come through that the ship was to return to Portsmouth to be paid off. The thought of their departure made me feel a little bleak, and then quite without warning I was told I was to go with them.

I did not then realise what a unique privilege this was and that it had only been gained by great effort and persistence, for it was against every naval regulation for anyone in my condition to be carried in an operational ship and if anything had gone wrong there would have been serious trouble for those responsible.

I rather dreaded being got aboard as, not long before, I had seen a man lowered in a stretcher from the crane and it had been done so carelessly that he had nearly been tipped into the water.

I almost suffered the same fate from the opposite reason because the Captain, Commander and Torpedo Officer were all yelling different instructions to the driver of the crane at the same time. I felt that with my plastered legs I should have sunk without trace.

My plasters had begun to stink revoltingly and when on deck my friends were careful to keep windward of me.

Not only the Captain but the Commander had been replaced. We missed our old friend and speculated as to what tall stories he was telling about our ship and the heroic roles he had played in the very minor actions in which we had been involved. I was able to catch up with what had been happening in my absence. I had not been replaced as chaplain and there were many complaints about the priests who had come aboard to take services.

I was fascinated at the great indignation there was throughout the ship about a Chaplain who had refused to wear vestments. This had no ecclesiastical significance whatever, I regret to say, but was no more than a certain resentment against regular Chaplains. There were very few of these who would take a line against vestments, but his action had been interpreted as a lack of interest. Those present had reported: 'He couldn't be bothered to make things nice for the boys.' I was surprised that this had stirred up those who had never been near the chapel and it was considered that he just threw on a surplice implying: 'Anything will do for sailors.'

When Sunday came while we were at sea I could not bear that there should be no Mass aboard so I had myself carried up to the chapel and sat with my legs propped on either side of a card table which I used as an altar, thus forstalling by many years the now usual arrangement of churches!

There was the largest turn-out of communicants I had ever seen since I joined the ship and I reflected sadly that the best way to persuade people to come to Holy Communion was to get oneself almost killed!

Most of the ship's company were the same men who had sailed away from Plymouth almost three years before and now we were going home over the same route with the war over and a store of common memories which would last us for the rest of our lives. As we sailed up the coast of Portugal we were fairly close to the shore and, through a pair of binoculars, I

127

was able to see the great palace-monastery of Santarem, where the King and Queen used to play at being monks having monastic cells as well as their royal apartments. I was filled with a great sadness for I wondered if I would ever be mobile enough to travel again in Europe and able to see these things which had such a fascination for me.

In 1950 I visited Portugal with a friend and one afternoon, without telling him where I was going, I took a bus from Lisbon to Santarem. As I sat having a drink in a café and looking up at the great church, I felt I had won a battle. If I had known five years before as I looked at it from the sea what a struggle lay ahead to get myself moving I should have been even more depressed.

We arrived at Portsmouth with our paying-off pennant streaming out behind the ship as we sailed into harbour. Wives and relatives were thick on the dockside and amongst them was my mother. I was saddened by how old she seemed to have become since I had last seen her, for her hair had turned completely white. I cannot have been a very cheerful sight myself for I was considerably wasted by malaria and had turned a bright yellow from the drug they gave me to keep it at bay. I had begun to lose a lot of hair and my legs now stank like polecats, so that it was no wonder that my mother burst into tears.

I said goodbye to my ship-mates and felt rather lonely as I was taken in a launch through driving rain to Hasler Hospital, a rather grim pile of buildings, on the other side of the harbour. As I was wheeled through the big wards the small groups of men in ill-fitting hospital blues, huddled round an ancient coke stove, looked like something out of Dicken's novels.

The room in which I was deposited had the same old-fashioned flavour. The fire smoked so badly that they let it go out. When the Surgeon-Captain did his rounds he said: 'Good God! the man has just come from the tropics, do you want him to freeze to death?' When the sister said that the chimney smoked he barked: 'Then get a sweep.' They did and he came in the middle of the night and I was covered with a white sheet like a corpse.

Jack Wilson came to see me. It had been a joke in our Eastney days to speak to each other in exaggerated sanctimonious tones of comic clergymen. I looked up from the paper I was reading and said: 'Have you seen, brother, that they propose to turn us out of our livings if we are cited as co-respondents in a divorce case?' He replied at once: 'Yes, I know, brother. It is just one more manifestation of that killjoy spirit which is so prevalent in the world today.' And immediately we were back in our old affectionate relationship, although he was now the Chaplain of the Fleet.

After he retired he went to be chaplain to a girls' school where I went to see him. 'I'm getting the hang of this job,' he said. 'yesterday I was doing some gardening with the girls who were eating the vegetables and one of them said: "I haven't had a pea since last year" and I never said a thing!'

I was examined by various doctors. They would take my X-rays over to the window, hold them up and mutter together. One of them let out a whistle when he saw the plates.

The orthopaedic specialist of the Navy, who was a Surgeon-Rear Admiral came to see me and talked at length about what they proposed to do about my left leg. When he suddenly changed his tone and said: 'Now, my dear boy,' I knew what he was going to say before he told me that my right leg must come off.

Before I joined the Navy I had said to a friend: 'I don't in the least mind being killed, but I simply couldn't bear to be mutilated.' The thing I had forgotten is that God always gives us the grace to bear anything which is laid upon us. I certainly experienced this vividly at that time and I hope it has taught me not to worry about the future.

People at once began to try to cheer me up. 'Of course you'll be able to dance', they all said. I longed to tell them that the only advantage I could see in having my leg removed was that it would give me a cast-iron excuse *not* to dance which, even as a young man, I had always found a crashing bore. A patient who had recently had an artificial limb was brought to encourage me. He sat talking for some time about all the things he found he could do. When he got up to leave he fell flat on his face!

The Rear Admiral had assured me that it would not interfere at all with my job, but I discovered that he had said to an almost totally disabled patient: 'Cheer up! You could always be a parson.'

It was decided that I should go to the Naval Orthopaedic

Hospital at Sherborne in Dorset to have my leg off, rather like being transferred to another prison for execution. The ambulance in which I travelled was obviously one of the Black Market suppliers for Portsmouth as we kept turning off the road to visit farms where I was given a cup of tea while every vacant space was filled with eggs and plucked fowls.

My first sight of the hospital at Sherborne was very dismal for it was a raw, bleak day and the long low buildings with a great chimney belching smoke made me feel that I had been brought to the gas chambers.

My reception reinforced this fantasy for the men who had brought me, anxious to get the booty back to Portsmouth, insisted that they must return everything I was wearing to Hasler, so they stripped me and left me naked. By the time the Sister discovered that I had arrived my teeth were chattering. She was furious with the Sick Berth Attendants who had shown no interest as they were, as usual, grumbling together about not being demobilised. She blasted them off to get hot bottles and pyjamas and I regained hope.

The officers' ward was being redecorated but we were soon moved back and I was given a room to myself with an enormous window on the ledge of which I was able to watch pots of bulbs sprout, grow tall and flower which was a strange experience as I had never before, and never since, had time to contemplate living things with undivided concentration.

The Ward Sister was a battle-axe of the highest order, whom I remember with amusement and affection, although at the time her edge sometimes seemed too sharp. Her life was dedicated to taking junior officers down a peg or two. She once said to me : 'When I see two and half stripes I know he'll need putting in his place.' Luckily she was an R.C. so she had a healthy respect for the cloth of any denomination.

She even terrorised the doctors and once when dressing my wounds said : 'I'm not going to put on this penicillin which the doctor is so fond of. I shall use Eusol, we had it in the first war and it heals better.' She had a syringe which looked as if it was for garden use, but against all reason she hurt one much less giving an injection than the tender-hearted V.A.D.s who had replaced the disgruntled Sick Berth Attendants.

I was allowed to have a good deal of morphia, but the Sister was very much against pain-killers of any kind and when any-

thing went wrong, for I had a lot of setbacks, she would say :
'It's all those pricks you've been having.'

Luckily the Night Sister was on my side and she would give
me drugs from another ward so that they were not recorded
in our book. 'There you are,' the Sister would say triumphantly
when she came on in the morning 'you can do without it if
you try'. Meanwhile I would be lying back contentedly doped.

On the morning of my operation, Alex Lawson, who had
come from Oxford to visit me, said Mass in my room and left
behind a set of vestments so that later I was able to say Mass
myself sitting on the edge of my bed and, when I was able to
get up, from a wheel chair in the ward. Not long ago a priest
gave me news of the schoolmaster in his parish. He told me that
we had been in hospital together. The schoolmaster was a keen
churchman, but had formerly been a Methodist. He told this
priest that the first thing which made him think of joining the
Church was when he had seen me saying Mass in a wheel chair.

The chaplain when I first arrived in the hospital had been a
great Moral Rearmament man. I tried to make my confession,
but it turned into a 'sharing session' and I found that he was
confessing to me. He was replaced by a splendid man who
could beat me hollow at talking. I was fascinated the first time
he came to visit me that when he left I had hardly managed
to get my oar in the water. I longed for him to return for the
next round and soon discovered a technique for getting a word
in.

He was a most amusing person with wide interests and an
enquiring mind which was completely unprejudiced so that he
was capable of adapting himself to any type of churchmanship.
He had changed his job every few years and had been a schoolmaster, an embassy chaplain, both an air force and naval
chaplain, a chaplain of the Missions to Seamen as well as
having been vicar of several parishes. His entry in *Crockford's
Clerical Directory* took up half a column.

I gave him *The Shape of the Liturgy* by Dom Gregory Dix
to read, as it was causing a great stir at that time and he declared
himself completely convinced by it. As a convert he was a
pushover.

There was no chapel in the hospital and so he took over the
Gas Decontamination Centre—which seemed a little super-
fluous by that time—and began to transform it. He came

bouncing into my room and said: 'I want you to help me make it look as Catholic as possible.' He had certainly found the right man! The Devon ladies, who had made things for the chapel of the *Ceylon* and whose needles had flagged a little since the war ended, made frontals and vestments. The friary at Cerne Abbas, which had a carpenter's shop, made a tabernacle and six large candlesticks. With the addition of a few little refinements, such as a holy water stoup and the Stations of the Cross, the effect was all that I could have wished. The Chaplain was responsible for the final touch which was a large board outside reading 'Chapel of St. Patrick'.

All went well till there was a change of Admirals and the new one proved to be a member of something called the Evangelical Group Movement. He sent for the Chaplain and said: 'I would like to know your religious views, Padre, because I don't think I approve of them.' The Chaplain was dumbfounded and came steaming along to me saying with indignation: 'I can't think why the man should start on me before he's even been to a service.' I said gently: 'Don't you think perhaps he's had a peep inside the chapel?'

In high dudgeon he at once applied for his discharge from the service on the grounds that he had been subjected to unwarranted interference with his work, and left before he and the admiral came to anything but a verbal battle. The chapel was dismantled and turned back into a Decontamination Centre —but by that time I had also left the hospital.

When I began to get about in a wheelchair I was taken for the first time into Sherborne Abbey, the fan vaulting of which excited me so much after almost a year in hospital wards that it kept me awake till the Night Sister gave me a knock-out sleeping daught. I was pushed out by various people including a boy from Sherborne School, who was the son of my housemaster and is himself today a distinguished headmaster. He wore a large flat straw hat which he was forced to keep on his head so that in a wind he had only one hand for the chair which I found very frightening on the steep hill of the main street.

I went to chapel often at Sherborne School, for the headmaster had a son who had served with me at Eastney Barracks. On most Sunday evenings I was collected and as the chapel was upstairs I was carried into it in a chair on the shoulders of the

132

boys like the pope. After chapel I was entertained in the head-master's house.

There were so many people in Sherborne who were kind to me and my memories of my time there are so warmed by friendship that I have forgotten the horrors of losing my leg. I am told that it was burned so that when people ask me for my opinion of cremation I always begin by saying: 'Well, I have a foot in both camps!'

The mother house of the Anglican Franciscans was not far away and I was visited by Fr. Algy Robertson. As I had mixed him up in my mind with Brother Douglas, whose tall ascetic figure I had seen at Oxford, I was very surprised when a small plump man, whose head did not come far above my very high bed, came bustling into my room.

Those who knew Fr. Algy will be amused that almost his first words were to ask if there was a telephone he could use. He then disappeared into the sister's office for half an hour. He seemed to live in a perpetual muddle and wherever he was ought to have been somewhere else, but he was like a little flame who left fires burning wherever he went up and down the country. Once when he was a minister at High Mass it was noticed with horror that a small trickle of water was appearing wherever he moved in the sanctuary. It was discovered that he had a hot water bottle tied round his waist under his habit and that it was leaking.

When I was better able to get around I used often to get myself taken to the Friary at Cerne Abbas. On my first visit I was carried into the parlour and had tea with the Friars, but when I was able to use crutches I would sometimes stay for the weekend.

Once, when all the priests of the community were out of the house on a Sunday evening, they wanted to have Solemn Even-song as it was the feast of St. Clare and so I obliged. It was not easy to cense an altar on crutches wearing a cope, but I did it!

I was able to exercise my ministry a little in the hospital and I prepared one of my fellow patients for confirmation. When the bishop came the service was held in the ward, but the chaplain did not tell him who was to be confirmed and so he presumed that it was the lot. I have never seen such frightened faces as he approached the first bed with hands outstretched.

They were obviously too terrified to speak and so I whizzed forward in my wheelchair and stopped a wholesale distribution of the Sacrament. I assured them afterwards that it would not have done them any harm!

I was fitted for an artificial limb in the Bishop's Palace at Exeter which was being used at that time by the Ministry of Pensions. A more unsuitable house for the disabled could not be imagined as it was full of dark passages and slippery steps. By this time I was dragging myself around on a full length calliper as my left leg had not set properly. If my crutches slipped I went down with a sickening thud upon my stump which made me almost vomit with pain.

The addition of a tin leg helped a bit, but my own showed few signs of mending. Doctors were by this time being demobilised at such a rate that I never quite knew who was in charge of my case—at one moment it was a specialist who was soon returning to his practise as a gynaecologist.

One of my fellow patients had an aunt who was a Hospital Matron and a great friend of Gaythorne Girdlestone, the founder of the Wingfield Orthopaedic Hospital in Oxford, and she was getting him transferred there. Through this rather indirect route Girdlestone heard about me and wrote saying that he would like to have me as a patient; but as he had had one or two brushes with the Navy he thought the best way to arrange things was to get the Bishop of Oxford to apply for me to be returned to the diocese. This ruse did not deceive the Surgeon-Captain for he said to me before I left : 'I hope it isn't Girdlestone who is behind this because he's a very tiresome old man and has caused us a lot of trouble before.' I said nothing as it was not asked in the form of a question. To be fair to the Navy, my condition was more complicated than Girdlestone thought and his assumption that he was just clearing up another mess they had made was somewhat premature.

To some people, G.R.G. as he was known, was a 'tiresome old man', because he could be very awkward and he hated red tape, but he was a great, wonderful and compassionate surgeon who gave himself to his patients with overwhelming generosity. He had trained in orthopaedics under the great pioneer Sir Robert Jones. During the Great War he was sent to open a hospital at Headington, on the hill above Oxford. It began as a collection of huts, but when the war was over he refused to let it

134

die and with the help of William Morris, later Lord Nuffield, he built up a world-famous orthopaedic centre.

He worked very largely by instinct which made it difficult for him to pass on his knowledge. He was a deeply religious man and would always pray before performing an operation firmly believing that he received help and guidance in this way. After I left hospital and was living in Oxford he would sometimes ring me up and say: 'If you are going to church this morning I should be grateful for your help as I have got rather a tricky operation and I don't know quite what to do for the best.'

The Wingfield Hospital had developed very much an atmosphere of its own and to become a patient there was like joining a club. In orthopaedics there is so often a bit more that needs to be done which means that the same people returned frequently and it was said as a joke: 'Once a Wingfield patient always a Wingfield patient.'

Most of the Sisters had worked with G.R.G. for many years and knew his ways. Nothing pleased him more than to be able to slip into a ward and do his rounds without the Sister knowing he was there and before the breakfast things had been cleared away. Yet in other ways he could be very temperamental and make things difficult for he was a highly strung man and in some ways painfully shy. He was very fond of talking about 'the Wingfield spirit', but no one could kill it more effectively than he when he was in the wrong mood.

He didn't find it easy to make contact with people and there were some who found him a very frightening person; but from the start I discovered a delightful and affectionate friend who took me very much into his confidence. When he died suddenly I was surprised to discover that I was almost the only person to whom he had confessed the real state of his health.

The atmosphere of the Wingfield was very different from the Naval Hospital at Sherborne where 'the traditions of the Service' followed one to the edge of the grave. One of the Wingfield specialities was to give patients a lot of fresh air and it was claimed that glass doors had only been fitted to the open side of the wards after one of the nurses was found to be suffering from frostbite. I often had my bed out in the snow and very nice it was with stars glittering above if I kept all but my nose under the blankets. It was not so much fun if it began to rain and the night nurse was not on the spot. On one occasion we had to get ourselves under cover, the most mobile of us using his crutches as oars and the rest holding on to the end of each others' beds like a chain of elephants.

I was put into Nani Ward, named after an Arabian princess who had died of polio. It was intended for babies but during the war and after was used for officers. Sister Martin, one of the old G.R.G. brigade and a magnificent nurse, who was in charge of the ward said she found the problems much the same!

As I was back in Oxford I had a lot of visitors—one kind friend took me on a drive to see the crematorium on the day before I had an operation. It reminded me of the day on which I had my leg off when a gift arrived for me by the morning post before I was taken to the theatre—it was a book called *The Divine Crucible of Purgatory*.

The chapel at the Wingfield was something of a disappointment after the chapel of St. Patrick but nothing much happened in it and I seldom used it. The chaplain was a local vicar who had plenty to do in his parish and was assisted by a Deaconess I think we had a Communion about once a month and the Deaconess came to me the day before and said: 'Will you partake tomorrow, Mr. Stephenson?' I asked, rather suspiciously: 'Who will be bringing Communion?' and assured myself that it was the Vicar. Not long ago I did receive Holy Communion in a well-known Anglo-Catholic church from a woman. I could have avoided it by going to the other end of the altar rail where the curate was administering the chalice, but I felt that it would be too 'square'. However the same evening I was at a party where an actress began asking me a lot of very impertinent questions about my sex life and I said: 'I received Communion from a woman for the first time this morning and I have no intention of finishing the day by making my confession to one!'

On Sundays at the Wingfield we often had services in the ward taken by students from a low church theological college and for the first time in my life I was asked if I were saved. I replied: 'I hope I am in the process of being saved, but at the moment I feel that it is hard work!'

Everyone in the ward hated these services and complained so bitterly to the chaplain that he asked me if I would be prepared to take them myself. It was very testing to have to sit up in bed and preach at the companions with whom one had spent every moment of the previous week. I began to recite the Breviary again for I had plenty of time and found it a great consolation as it kept me firmly within the liturgical life of the church.

I had three operations at the Wingfield; one of them coincided with the terrible winter of 1947 and I watched the snow come and go, six weeks later, from my bed. Friends used to come and visit me in order to get warm as hospitals were exempt from the power cuts which took place at that time. In between the operations I had what we called 'plaster leave' which I spent with my mother, who had recently moved into a flat on the New Church Road in Hove.

I found the respectability of Hove depressing and much preferred the rakishness of Brighton next door, but my movements were very restricted. It was then that I got an electric invalid carriage, having started with one which looked like a dentist's chair on wheels but soon getting a new and efficient model. This gave me my first feeling of independence and I could go off on my own without assistance from anyone. I had been in hospital for so long that I sometimes wondered if I should ever fit into ordinary life again. I can remember at Sherborne getting myself to the hospital gates in a wheel chair and feeling quite frightened by the cars flashing past.

I went to church at St. Martin's, Brighton, when I was at home and sat entranced at the lengthy eloquence of its vicar, Fr. Colin Gill, as he preached from a pulpit built on the same handsome proportions as himself. When in full spate he sometimes looked as if he might do one a mischief if he could get out. Once I was needed as a minister at Solemn Adoration, but I had promised to preach at the Church of the Annunciation so Colin Gill simply said: 'I'll just keep preaching till you arrive.' And he did! I may add that the service at St. Martin's began at 6 p.m. and the one at the Annunciation at 6.30 p.m.

St. Martin's was a wonderful church and in those days full of life—not quite as high as Bart's in size, but overtopping it in churchmanship. The tragedy has been that it has seemed impossible to keep all the Brighton churches flourishing at the same time and someone said to me not long ago: 'No one has been converted in Brighton for the last fifty years and the Catholics just regroup themselves around the churches in a sort of General Post every few years.'

Mother Sarah of Laleham bought a house in Rottingdean at this time as a holiday home for the Sisters. She called at my mother's flat with three of the Sisters, largely it transpired to use the W.C. I got quite hysterical sitting with them in the drawing room while she said to them one by one : 'Sister would you care to go and see Mrs. Stephenson?' For a long time afterwards I teased my mother by saying : 'I'm just going to see Mrs. Stephenson.'

I gave Mother Sarah a lot of the vestments I had used in the Navy to help furnish the chapel at Rottingdean and would often go along the under-cliff path in my electric chair and say Mass there. If the Reverend Mother was in residence we would sit after breakfast on the verandah in the sun while she talked to me about the sorrows and difficulties of her life and I warmed to her considerably.

It was during one of these quiet talks that I persuaded her to make up the feud which had developed between herself and Hope Patten at Walsingham after he had tried to hi-jack some of her nuns. I was able to assure him from what Mother Sarah said to me that he would not be snubbed if he made an approach and he visited Laleham again, so there was 'peace in our time'.

I was longing to do a proper job and a chance came when a chaplain was needed for a community of nuns who had established themselves in the disused Bishop's Palace at Cuddesdon where they lived under the surprised gaze of the eighteenth-century Bishop's of Oxford, whose portraits still looked down on them.

The most convenient arrangement would have been for the staff of the theological college which was opposite to have acted as chaplains; but it did not work very well in practice as none of them understood much about the needs of enclosed nuns and tended to behave as if they were female theological students—lecturing them about the Book of Common Prayer.

Bishop Kirk came to their rescue and pointed out that the B.C.P. never envisaged the possibility of religious communities and was entirely unsuitable for their use. It did seem rather bizarre to give them nothing but Ante-communion with the Ten Commandments on Holy Saturday.

I was very lame, but my leg had been taken out of plaster and the Wingfield Hospital was not far away so that I could go daily for treatment. When I arrived at the convent the two

Wantage nuns who had been lent to direct the new community said to me: 'Perhaps we had better begin by telling you about ourselves—I'm Juste and she's Rebe.' I was tempted to say: 'I hope you'll both be better soon.'

It was very interesting to see a community at its birth and this, for many reasons, was a particularly hard labour, but I was not able to stay with them long as the leg broke down and, having dragged myself around long passages of the enormous house in agony for a few weeks, I was forced to return to hospital. It did however forge a link with the Sisters and after they had moved to Burford Priory and adopted the rule of St. Benedict, as I was by that time in Oxford, I was able to assist at the solemn profession of the first Sisters and their canonical enclosure.

Alex Lawson, after bidding fair to be a life-long curate, had been given the living of St. Ives in Huntingdonshire and I went to help him during the first Holy Week there, when he put on all the ceremonies for the first time. On Good Friday the Mass of the Pre-Sanctified was punctuated by the slamming of the church door as each successive portion of the rite proved too much for the various members of the congregation. On Holy Saturday, having spent almost three hours in the consecration of the New Baptismal Water, the old verger pulled the plug out of the font and emptied it all away.

I was offered a living myself at this time which was not far from Walsingham and although I was still a hospital patient I felt that I must go and see it. I was told in awed tones by the Rural Dean that 'an Anglo-Catholic woman' lived in the parish.

It was a tiny parish and the old churchwarden said: 'We do hope the new vicar won't visit quite as much as the last one did.' In fact I had to refuse the living for in the event I still had a long time to do in hospital before I was discharged, but in any case although I did not know how mobile I might be, I felt I ought to be able to do more than act as private chaplain to one Anglo-Catholic woman in the wilds of Norfolk.

I went to the Shrine at Walsingham several times and after being sprinkled at the Holy Well I put away my crutches determined that I would walk without their aid. With God's help and Our Lady's prayers I have managed to do so, except on rare occasions when my stump has been so sore I have been unable to wear my artificial leg.

As the end of my time in hospital drew near I had to decide what I would do. I had become convinced that I ought to try my vocation as a monk and join my cousin at Nashdom, but things did not work out like that.

Fr. Hack, the Vicar of St. Mary Magdalen, Oxford, died and the patrons of the living, Christ Church, told the churchwardens that they did not consider the church to have much future sandwiched as it was between St. Giles and St. Michael-at-the-Northgate. A small but determined band dedicated themselves to keeping the church open and its Catholic tradition unchanged. They worked themselves into such a militant frame of mind that they used their legal powers to refuse the nomination of a very suitable priest whom the patrons presented. It was ironical that they gave as their objection that he had only one leg and they considered that he would not be active enough! The patrons felt rightly aggrieved and allowed the nomination to lapse to the bishop.

It was at this time that I had a letter from Bishop Kirk asking me to come and see him at the House of Lords. Their Lordships were debating the abolition of the death penalty and the old backwoodsmen peers were roving the chamber thirsting for blood. At last the Bishop of Oxford came out and said: 'I think we have got time now to talk; the Bishop of — is on his feet, he speaks at length and with great eloquence which disguises the fact that he hardly makes sense.'

He then told me of the situation at St. Mary Magdalen and how he thought I was the one person who might reconcile the parish and the patrons as I seemed to be acceptable to both. I told him that I was considering trying my vocation as a monk and he said: 'Please don't accept St. Mary Magdalen and then in six months tell me you want to leave and go off to Nashdom.' I promised that if I accepted I would stay for at least five years.

I had no idea what an agony it would be to make up my mind. Nashdom Abbey kindly agreed to take me as an Oblate Brother and I finally wrote to the Bishop accepting his offer—then stayed awake all night in a horrid fright that I had done the wrong thing. Officially I was still in the Navy and as I had a lot of leave due to me before I was discharged I was still in the Service when I was inducted as Vicar of St. Mary Magdalen's.

My left leg had mended after a final and drastic operation

by G.R.G. when he more or less pulled it apart and stuck one end of the bone up inside the other. Once when I had despaired of it ever joining I had suggested that he take it off leaving me as a double amputee, he had put his hand on my shoulder and said : 'I promise you I'll fix that leg if it's the last thing I do on earth.'

After I was settled in Oxford he would often telephone me and say : 'I saw you belting down Cornmarket today and I think you are doing too much on *our* leg.' When he discharged me from the hospital he said : 'Now go and burn yourself up in Christ's service, but do it very slowly and very wisely.'

10

Oxford Again

———————

As far as there is any record I am the first Vicar of St. Mary Magdalen, Oxford who has been silly enough to resign! They have all decayed gently and died in office, while I felt my leaving like another amputation, but that was ten years after I unlocked the door, rang the bell and performed all the other palaver of solemn nonsense which is called a Service of Induction.

The Bishop of Oxford preached from the text: 'The Lord hath brought me home,' (Ruth 1 : 21) and this certainly expressed what I felt as I gazed at the large congregation made up of friends from all over the city.

The parish has an interesting history as it was the first church built outside the city walls to serve the riff-raff, many of whom were harlots (hence its dedication), who were not allowed to live inside. The Royal Palace of Beaumont was down near the later Worcester College and Edward II gave it to the Carmelites who built a chapel on the south side of St. Mary Magdalen. The narrow lane called Friars Entry opposite the church still shows their route of access.

Balliol College still pays the Vicar of St. Mary Magdalen an annual rent based on the number of resident undergraduates, which dates from their foundation in the fourteenth century when they used a chantry on the north side of the church as their chapel dedicated to St. Catherine.

As vicar I found myself also Custodian of the Martyrs Memorial which had been erected in what was then the churchyard as a counterblast to the teachings of the Oxford Movement. Generations of undergraduates had climbed it leaving an article of bedroom furniture on the top as a record of their feat. During my incumbency some young men were caught having pulled a pinnacle or two down in their attempt and I had to discuss with the Proctors what measure could be taken to protect the Memorial. I said: 'Could not a referendum be taken in the University to find out the number of undergraduates who would like to see a jerry-pot on the top, and, if it proves a large number, one could be cemented on.' The Senior Proctor said reprovingly: 'I sense a point of view coming out, Fr. Stephenson.'

All the extending north and south gave the church its very curious shape; standing as it does on an island surrounded by roads, it is wider than it is long. In fact it contrives to be very convenient in use as no one can get very far away from the altar; and, having four separate aisles, makes a fairly small weekday congregation feel a certain 'togetherness' which one lacks in a longer building from the maddening propensity of English people to sit at the back if they get the chance.

At the beginning of this century the vicar was Canon Clayton, a great figure in Oxford in more senses than one as he weighed over twenty stone. His nickname was 'Tubby' which was inherited by his nephew who was the founder of Toc H.

He was vicar for over thirty years and they were the great days of churchgoing. It was then that Mary Corbett was the 'pew-opener', her father being the parish clerk. She lived to tend the votive candle stands and answer Mass in Fr. Hack's days when she gave the church an authentic continental air for she was an exact replica of the old women one used to see doing the same thing in French churches. She was still alive in an old people's home when I became vicar, for her tiny house in Friars' Entry had been pulled down. She was a hoarder and never threw anything away. Alex once found her stuffing old candle ends into jam jars and rebuking her said: 'I like everything to be simple,' to which she replied quietly 'I'm very surprised to hear it'—which showed that her wits were not so dull as some people were tempted to think.

Basil Blackwell, the bookseller, once said to me: 'I suffered terrible things in your church as a boy, for Canon Clayton was the longest and dullest preacher I have ever had to endure.' There must however have been excitements during his sermons for I have been told that he was in the habit of descending from the pulpit and giving the cane to a choirboy he had observed misbehaving and then returning to read from his script as if nothing had happened.

He died towards the end of the Great War and his place was taken by Mr. Gilkes, who had been a lay headmaster of Dulwich and wished to do some war work on his retirement. Having been told there was a shortage of clergy he had himself ordained and was at once given the living of St. Mary Magdalen. He did not remain a 'makee-learn' for long as he dropped dead suddenly in the Broad when he had been vicar for less than two years. He died outside No. 53, which was the house he had obtained as the Vicarage by a straight swop with the city who in exchange took over the disused church of St. George, a mission church situated on Gloucester Green where the cinema now stands.

After Gilkes' death Christ Church appointed as vicar in his place the very high incumbent of another of their Oxford livings, St. Thomas the Martyr. His name was Bartle Starmer Hack. He had never been really happy at St. Thomas' as he was overshadowed by his predecessor Birley who had gone off to Central Africa and became Bishop of Zanzibar. The old ladies were always comparing him unfavourably with 'dear Mr. Birley' whom they thought far less a 'romanist' than their new vicar.

The day came when the newly consecrated Bishop of Zanzibar returned to preach and Hack was somewhat amused, and the old ladies chagrined, that he had stopped in Marseilles en route and had himself fitted out, appearing in church in a purple biretta and mozetta like a Roman prelate.

Hack was only a 'romanist' in his love of baroque vestments and ornaments. No one could have more disliked the title 'Father'. 'Nasty Roman Catholic habit', he would say disapprovingly, and yet he was known as Fr. Hack by everyone in Oxford —dons, college porters, people in shops as well as his own congregation. He always wore a frock coat for he considered it an impropriety for a priest to show his bottom and he liked to think of himself as a Tractarian with Dr. Pusey as his model. Every day his portly figure could be seen walking down the Cornmarket with a pile of books under his arm. It was commonly thought that like the learned Doctor, he read the Fathers for recreation but in fact he was an avid reader of novels and got through six a day, so that he was usually on his way to Boots Lending Library. Later he would be seen from the Broad sitting under a lamp in his drawing room, for he scorned electric light, and deeply absorbed in what he was reading. Those who saw him were convinced that it was the works of St. Ambrose, but it was more likely to be the works of Miss Ethel M. Dell which were holding his attention.

His enormous belly must have reminded his parishioners of Canon Clayton, particularly when he preached on 'Fasting' at the beginning of Lent as he heaved it on to the edge of the pulpit. There was a story told of a woman dropping her handkerchief into his lap on a bus. She was too embarrassed to retrieve it but Hack could see her looking at something; to her horror he firmly tucked it inside his trousers as he thought it was his shirt sticking out.

They must also have been reminded of the Canon when someone asked Hack sentimentally what he would put into a 'Children's Corner' and he replied sharply : 'A birch rod.' He could indeed be very sharp in rebuke and once stopped in the middle of a sermon and said to a woman who was fidgeting : 'Either shut that handbag or leave the church.'

His greatest source of irritation was people who left the church door open when they came in and he would rebuke them at once from the pulpit, or confessional and even from the altar if they paused on the threshold. One day a young man who had just finished his confession said timidly : 'I'm afraid that it was I who left the door open.' The waiting penitents were horrified to hear a loud voice from the box say : 'That is the unforgiveable sin.'

He is chiefly remembered in Oxford for complaining about the hill in the Broad which he claimed to find very trying when walking to church—those who do not know Oxford will fail to appreciate the joke without being told that there is an almost imperceptible rise in the ground in front of Trinity College.

Someone who knew the church before Hack became vicar described it to me as 'a dreary little preaching box'. It smelt strongly of gas and was packed out with pews. Hack introduced vestments at once, popping a biretta on his head and saying : 'They might as well have the whole dose in one go.' In other ways he went very slowly and he kept Matins at eleven till the beginning of the last war. When no one turned up, they were all listening to the Prime Minister's speech, he said: 'Well, that finishes that', and he never had it again.

For many years he had been building up a Sung Mass at ten at which everything must conform strictly to the Prayer Book, although the ornaments and ceremonial were completely baroque. He would never even insert 'The Lord be with you' because it was not in the Prayer Book and he always recited the Ten Commandments. Yet he said Mass in such a completely objective way that often Roman Catholics would attend and not know that they had not been at a Latin Mass.

He didn't really like having a congregation and never made any effort that they should hear what was being said. Often before Evensong in the winter he would go round before the service saying: 'There won't be many here this evening, why don't you slip home'—he would then be left to say the Office and read Dr. Pusey's sermons to Mary Corbett which was what he liked best.

Little by little he altered the interior of the church, removing the pews and restoring altars at the ends of the aisles. He brought back candlesticks and chandeliers from Bruges which was a city he loved and where he frequently went on holiday. When Alex Lawson became his curate the pace quickened and the beautiful image of Our Lady of Joy was put in the church. Alex persuaded him that the aumbry might make the Holy Sacrament go mouldy and so he allowed a tabernacle on the altar of the Lady Chapel while Alex turned the aumbry into a Shrine of the Sacred Heart. But while he would let Alex do more or less what he liked in adorning the church, he made him conform to the Prayer Book when he said Mass, never allowing the Creed or Gloria to be omitted, even during Lent or at requiems.

I got to know him quite well at the beginning of the war, when I was a curate at SS. Mary & John, for Alex and I would often take him on expeditions stopping for lunch at some country hotel as he was fond of food and found the wartime restrictions very disagreeable. He would study the menu carefully and then he would say with his eyes sparkling: 'I think we've struck oil.'

I noticed at dinner parties he would make animated conversation to his neighbours on either side the moment he sat down to table, but once the food appeared he would concentrate his whole attention on it and not utter a word.

146

On one of our expeditions we went to look at the Pugin Roman Catholic church at Buckland. As we came up the path the Romish clergyman was standing at the door trying to make out what we were—Hack in a frock coat, Alex in a black suit and I in a soutane. He asked, rather rudely: 'Protestant or Catholic?' Hack simply replied: 'Established' and walked into the church without another word.

Once at the Oxford Ruri-decanal Chapter we had someone to talk on 'The Place of Women in the Church' which Hack listened to with ill-disguised impatience. The Rural Dean was unwise enough to ask him what he thought on the subject, to which he replied: 'As far as I know there is only one place for women in the church and that is on their knees—praying or scrubbing and there is plenty of use for both.'

He strongly suspected that the undergraduate bell-ringers took women up the tower with them, but he was too fat to get up and see, so he refused to begin the Mass saying to the server: 'They have got a Jezebel up that tower, but I'll give her a flea in her ear when she comes down.'

Sometimes I would draw his attention to the somewhat decayed fabric of the church and he would say: 'It'll last my time and my successor can see to all that.' Neither of us had any idea that it was his successor to whom he was speaking.

He was vicar for nearly twenty years but during the war things rather ran downhill for there were no buses on Sundays and there were very few people left living in the parish, which was mostly made up of shops, offices and cinemas, so the congregation dwindled badly. It was lucky that he had never much cared for having people in church, but he was a confessor of great skill and perception and those who thought the church should be closed did not realise the flock of penitents who frequented the confessional there.

Death overtook him when he was talking of retirement. After the funeral Alex wrote to the Bishop of Dorchester apologising for his behaviour which had been somewhat brusque, as he had begun Mass while the bishop was still trying to have a ceremonial reception at the west door. He wrote: 'The modern Roman Catholic ceremonial surrounding a prelate, which I myself prefer and which has become common in this diocese was abhorrent to Fr. Hack and was contrary to his wishes.' Hack had in fact said to Alex: 'Once I'm dead don't you get out your Roman Missal and say, "He knows better now", because I shan't!'

By the time I came to St. Mary Magdalen, because of the delay in making an appointment, Hack had been dead for over a year and they had had an exciting interregnum during which the vicar's warden (a protégé of Alex's) who was in charge had ridden them hard towards Rome. It must be the only church in the country which has had the ceremonies of the Triduum Sacrum introduced while the living was vacant.

The congregation was not very large, but the small group who had fought for the survival of the church had found a unity of purpose which made them a really solid foundation on which to build.

One of the most strong-minded was an artist, Elfrida Llewellyn-Davies, who had a neurotic and excitable dog called Gregory at which she was always taking a swipe and once hit me by mistake. I loved her dearly because I could always tell her to 'shut up' without her taking the least offence. Therefore I was terribly saddened when I was told she had a cancer which was likely to cause her severe pain before it killed her for I was so afraid it would break that wonderful spirit. She went through a miserable time, but took the news that she had no chance of recovery as if she had been told she was to move house. At last I was sent for in a hurry and she was in great pain and could only gasp : 'I'm dying, give me the Last Sacraments.' I took a little time getting out the Holy Oils and a voice came from the bed : 'Hurry up, hurry up, I shan't last.' I was so encouraged that Frida was able to go down to the grave bossing me till the last moment, for she died as I was saying 'Go forth in peace, Christian Soul'.

The congregation had had so many changes during the past year that I could do more or less as I wished and so on the first Sunday I put the Gloria at the beginning of the Mass and the Our Father within the Canon, which had become the common practice in the more 'advanced' Anglo-Catholic churches. It is interesting that even then this was regarded as rather 'extreme' and to some legalists seemed very disloyal to the Prayer Book, while today it is the norm in all the new rites given sanction by Convocation.

On the first Sunday at St. Mary Magdalen when I intoned the Gloria in its new position my heart missed a beat for the immediate reaction was as if the entire congregation had stood up and were blowing 'raspberries' at me. It was the Salvation Army band which had struck up outside at that very moment! In fact it would have been hard to find a congregation less interested in the minutiae of Catholic procedure; one Sunday when we did not use incense because we had run out of charcoal not one person even mentioned it.

It was wonderful to have such a free hand, for St. Mary Magdalen represented the sort of church of which I had always dreamed. It had a very romantic medieval background so that I was able to restore many of its ancient customs—ringing the bells on the feast of St. Hugh, who had himself consecrated the south aisle in honour of St. Thomas of Canterbury; beating the bounds after the High Mass on Ascension Day; keeping the feast of Our Lady of Mount Carmel and restoring an image of St. Anne which it was recorded once stood in the Lady Chapel.

It was very like my youthful dreams and almost at once it began to draw a congregation of considerable size as if to prove my immature thesis that one had only to display the externals of baroque catholicism to draw folk to appreciate it at once.

Where did they all come from? As the church filled up so quickly I cannot, alas, claim that it was hard work on my part. I think what happened was that, being already known in Oxford, quite a lot of people came on the first few Sundays as a gesture of kindness towards me. Then word got round that St. Mary Magdalen's had suddenly become rather full and some of the unattached came to see what it was all about and the congregation gradually built up.

About this time one of the churches in North Oxford was going through a difficult period. The vicar was changing everything from Roman to Sarum usage—he had been nicknamed by his congregation 'Nightshirt Ned'. He became seriously unbalanced by the death of his aged mother, even wearing her jewellery in the pulpit and dissolving into floods of tears as he mentioned her in every sermon. His congregation found it very hard to bear and many began to go to other churches. While they did not by any means all come to St. Mary Magdalen's, quite a number found refuge there and became very useful to the church.

A number of undergraduates too suddenly began to consider

'Mary Mags' rather smart and in the curious way in which nothing succeeds like success, there were soon quite a lot of them to fill the odd corners. It was amusing, remembering my own undergraduate days, to have young men trying to 'spike me up' and thinking I was very square-toed because I would not 'whole hog' it as far as they wanted to push me.

To me the great charm of the congregation was that it had none of the stiffness and correctness found in many Anglican churches. They stood and sat as they felt inclined and if they were late had no inhibitions about coming up to the front, while if anything amused them they just laughed. I remember how upset a preacher for the Diocese of Gibraltar was when, having said that he knew many Italians who longed to join the Church of England, he was greeted with a gale of laughter.

There is something reassuring to English people about Gothic architecture and I discovered many people prepared to accept things at St. Mary Magdalen's which they thought too 'extreme' in the drawing-room setting of St. Paul's, Walton Street. When I was bemoaning the closure of this charming church it was said to me : 'You did more to kill it than anyone by starting another church with the same sort of religion, and there was only room for one church of that kind in Oxford'; and I fear there is much truth in that charge.

We were so lucky in having a perfect position in the centre of the city and on a bus stop. The entrance was right on the street so that people only had to take a few steps and they were inside the church. This is why it was always so full of people praying before the Sacrament and the Shrine of Our Lady of Joy ablaze with votive candles—vastly increased in numbers when the undergraduates were taking their examinations!

I have always felt that people ought to enjoy the worship of God and the secret of St. Mary Magdalen's was that they did. We were not inhibited by restraint and when there was a festival only the most obtuse person putting their head through the door could fail to notice that something special was going on, even if it were only from the green herbs scattered all over the aisles, their smell fortified by a bottle of Bay Rum which I had sprinkled on top of them.

A small girl, whose development was slightly arrested, had been accustomed by her parents to staying the length of the Sung Mass. At Christmas they took her to the pantomime and after two hours she gave a deep sigh and said: 'Oh dear this is much longer than Fr. Stephenson's church!'

One of my first problems was the music. We had a talented organist but not many people to do the singing. The answer was the result of a remarkable coincidence. While I was living in Hove with my mother I received a letter by mistake which had been intended for a nonconformist minister of the same name. I returned the letter to the sender in Oxford; it was about arrangements for a concert, and she replied very kindly thanking me and saying that if I ever needed anyone to sing she would be glad to help. At that time the possibility seemed very remote, but I kept the letter and when I looked at it the address was in Wellington Square, which was only just outside my new parish.

I went to call on the lady who was a teacher of singing and she was as good as her promise and not only came to sing herself, but brought several of her friends and pupils so that before long St. Mary Magdalen's had the best singing of any parish church in Oxford. To my regret we were never able to have an orchestra, but this was from lack of space and not of talent!

I developed the tradition, which Fr. Hack had started, of having a lot of late Masses which I felt sure was the right thing for a city church, and which proved to be so by the large numbers who came to Mass at that time. In the country around it was known that there was always a Mass at 11.15 a.m. and most of the congregation had shopping baskets. My successor has taken the logical step and also has an evening Mass every day which is attended by those who work in the city and like to go to Mass before setting off for their homes.

I was determined to have a lot of things going on in the church and I put down times for confession every day and not only at the end of the week, as in most churches. Someone said to me: 'I shall never forget the first time I went into St. Mary Magdalen's, there were two priests hearing confessions, a Mass was being said at one of the altars, and there was Exposition of the Blessed Sacrament in the Lady Chapel!' This was indeed the sort of church I had dreamed about when I was a boy.

I was lucky to get a lot of help from retired priests living in Oxford and from college chaplains. Pusey House was in the parish and the Principal and Librarians were always ready to help. Austin Farrer lived almost opposite the church and would always lend a hand, allowing himself to be dressed up in lace and pushed about the sanctuary—which was necessary as whenever he did not know what to do he shut his eyes and stood still. He was not the only great theologian who was prepared to help in our rather 'way out' church, and sometimes there would be four or five Doctors of Divinity in the congregation.

Cuthbert Simpson, first as Professor of Hebrew and later as Dean of Christ Church often said Mass for me and I treasure the memory of his rich American voice saying to me, when I was fussing on Holy Saturday: 'All right, take it easy, it's going very nicely', and swinging round to the Sub-Deacon 'and you can take it easy too.' Once when the organist had given him too high a note he said: 'What does he think I am, a bloody canary?'

He had a divine impatience which did not suffer fools gladly. A taxi driver stopped at the gates of Christ Church and said: 'The Dean doesn't like us to drive inside.' A voice from the back said: 'I am the bloody Dean!'

As an almost permanent assistant I had a sweet old priest who had spent his quiet life as curate in most of the fair-sized country towns around Oxford without ever having had a living of his own. To my great good fortune he retired to live in a boarding house in the parish and was prepared to say as many Low Masses as I wished and to sit in the confessional for hours. Nothing would persuade him either to preach or sing a note, but he exercised a wonderful ministry and his transparent goodness shone through everything he did. He was completely without ambition and would have much disliked my mentioning him by name, but in spite of his mildness he had a will of iron and nothing could persuade him to change his set habits. He would always take his own purificator home after saying Mass to wash himself; this almost drove the lady sacristan wild, but she never got it away from him.

It was typical that when he was dying with an obstruction in his throat the sister said: 'Isn't it wonderful, you have just managed to swallow some water?' He replied calmly: 'But I don't care for Oxford water.'

Undoubtedly the most colourful of my honorary assistants was Bishop Roscow Shedden who had been Bishop of Nassau and then returned home to be Vicar of Wantage. On his retirement he came to live in Woodstock and liked to call himself my 'curate'. He had been a remarkably handsome young man and even in old age he was a wonderful sight in pontifical vestments. He never really ceased to be the rather overbearing, lovable prefect he must have been at school, who always thought he could get his own way by shouting. And what a voice he had! At the time of the Anglo-Catholic Congress of 1933, in which he took part, a limerick was composed:

'There once was a prelate called Roscow
Who loved to say "nosco" and "posco"
Which he used to repeat
On episcopal seat
In a voice like the big bell of Moscow.'

I heard many tales about his voice when I visited the Bahamas for he would stand on the lawn of his house and call down to his bosun in the harbour and be audible all over town. He seemed entirely unable to modulate his voice and was apt to make what he thought to be quiet asides which would ring throughout the church. Once in the middle of reciting the Angelus he said: 'I shall want lavatory accommodation after this,' in exactly the same tone.

When visiting the out islands in his diocese he would stand up in his yacht and shout: 'The bishop's here', and the islanders would come trembling down to the beach to receive him with holy fear. He once asked an old catechist how many confirmation candidates he had and received the astonishing reply: 'Oh my Lord, I had a dozen, but they have been eaten by rats.' It transpired that the old man thoroughly frightened by the visitation thought the bishop had said 'candles'.

On another occasion he was pontificating at a church in Nassau and barking orders he said: 'Mitre', to a small boy holding it. He repeated the word with growing impatience and then said: 'Put it on boy', and the small boy solemnly put it on his own head! I knew the mitre only too well as it had a lot of metal decoration on the top and I have more than once nearly lost my eye when he wanted it off and butted at me like a goat. He once got it caught in the tassel hanging from the sanctuary lamp and began to shake his head like an angry bull so that the whole thing—glass, oil and all—upset over him adding to his rage.

He loved the music of St. Mary Magdalen's and when pontificating would get himself settled on the fald stool, his golden mitre on his head, take a large pinch of snuff with purple-gloved fingers, and then sit back with his eyes closed and a look of beatific contentment on his face.

He had mellowed a lot in old age for when he first went out to Nassau he took the Archdeacon by the throat and shook him bellowing: 'Your blasted incompetence is ruining the diocese.' But he was still able to show impatience as when leaving the altar at Candlemas with a candle in one hand and leaning heavily on a walking stick with the other, some old ladies knelt for his blessing and he snapped angrily: 'Get up, can't you see I haven't got a hand to bless you with!'

The choir could never get used to his going on with the Elevation of the Host while they were still singing the Sanctus for, like time and tide, he would wait for no man. We all loved him and when he died, which he managed to do in the W.C. behind the door of which was found his pastoral staff, we gave him the most elaborate Requiem possible, the choir singing Mozart which he loved above all things.

When I first moved back to Oxford I went to live at 53 Broad Street which was a large and dilapidated house opposite the Sheldonian Theatre which had become the last private residence left in the Broad. Trinity College and Blackwells were both very eager to acquire it as it lay between their properties. I made it clear that I should be willing to do a deal with whichever one could find me another house which I liked in the parish. After a good deal of negotiation Trinity produced a charming house in Beaumont Street which became the Vicarage, and I moved there after about a year in the Broad where I had the house full of undergraduate lodgers who sometimes made such a racket that I said: 'My final humiliation will be when they send in from the pub next door to ask if there can be less noise in the Vicarage!'

Fifteen, Beaumont Street became my home and was a very attractive house with a garden full of lovely scented plants tumbling over the walls which was cared for by a dear friend and parishioner who was a wizard with growing things and, fortunately for me, lived in a flat where she had no garden of her own.

I usually had undergraduates living with me in the house and at the end of each year I would say 'Never again', but I always did and would have felt very lonely without them. I had a wonderful housekeeper who was not only one of the best cooks

154

I have ever known but of a completely equable temperament. Once when the kitchen chimney caught fire she calmly stood at the sink doing the washing up while firemen carried out pails of flaming soot.

In many ways this was the happiest time of my life. Every year I managed to go to the Continent for my holidays and got to know large areas of France, Italy and Greece very well. After I had been in the parish for five years I took five months off and went to South Africa to take part in a mission in Johannesburg and Pretoria returning up the East Coast of Africa and seeing something of the work of the Universities Mission, of which I was the Oxford secretary, and about which I had known all my life as these dioceses were regarded as 'sound' by most extreme Anglo-Catholic parishes, although there was at least one Anglican church which would support nothing but the White Fathers' Mission.

Outside my back gate at Oxford were the stage doors of both the Playhouse and the New Theatre and I was Actors' Church Union chaplain to both. I could often be seen taking parties of chorus girls round the colleges on a sightseeing tour and, as I was usually wearing a cassock, I was sometimes the only one in a skirt. When an English version of the Folies Bergères came to Oxford I went backstage to see them, as I usually did on a Tuesday evening, and was surprised when two scantily clad young women rushed forward and embraced me with shrill cries of recognition. They were V.A.D.s who had nursed me in the Naval Hospital at Sherborne when I had my leg off. I suppose that I must have looked a little shy as they said: 'There's no need to be so cagey. We've seen far more of you than you can see of us!'

During the time of the pantomime we used to have a service in the theatre with members of the cast reading lessons and singing solos. One year the principal boy said she would like to sing 'The Nun's Song' which sounded all right to me, but to my horror proved to be a dramatic plea for deliverance of a girl shut up in a convent against her will. Fortunately her diction was so bad that few had any idea what she was singing about, but after this I always asked to see the words.

For this service the stage staff always took enormous trouble to produce a suitable set, usually like the interior of some exotic Spanish cathedral.

I had a tiny experience of being a country vicar, the thought of which had always held a fascination for me, although my more sober judgment made me realise that to be completely isolated in the country demanded an interior self-sufficiency I did not possess. I once said to a friend that I should like to be a hermit and he replied : 'Only in the middle of a brightly lighted stage.' Thank God for one's friends !

My small area of country parish was the care of the Water-eaton Chapel, an ancient chapel attached to the Manor House, the owners of which paid a chaplain to provide services for those living on the estate. It was a tiny community, but a parish in miniature and even had a branch of the Mothers' Union. One of the maids at the Manor stung by some disagreement said : 'I only ever joined to spite my auntie.'

It is impossible to write fully of a decade as a parish priest because it was so full of joys and sorrows and they were the joys and sorrows of my people. I can only say that I was conscious at the time that I had the most engaging church and the most affectionate and tolerant parishioners in England. I hope I was a good parish priest and I tried very hard to look after the people under my care, although I never really felt worthy of the love and affection which was poured out on me.

A church like St. Mary Magdalen was bound to have an ecletic congregation and I used to say sometimes that they were like the wind because of many 'I knew not whence they came nor whither they went'. There was a constant ebb and flow of people for Oxford is a place where they come to do a job and then go away. This continual change was in some ways very stimulating and prevented me from getting stale.

Every year there was a new intake of undergraduates and I always had very close contacts with some of them so that my house was constantly full of the young, many of whom are now ordained—a few have even risen to the purple. One distinguished diocesan bishop once came with a little bag of tools and mended my gas fire.

The congregations who gathered for Mass could not have been more varied in background. There were dons and their families, wealthy old ladies who lived in North Oxford, girls who worked in the shops and clerks and typists. There was a nice old road man who it was reported to me once said to a passer-by looking up from the leaves he was sweeping: 'You wouldn't think to look at me that I went to the highest church in Oxford!' And indeed I was delighted one day to hear a guide saying: 'And on your right, ladies and gentlemen, is the highest church in England'—he was pointing at St. Mary Magdalen. An undergraduate paper observed that 'if you go to St. Mary Magdalen a sidesman will hand you a Prayer Book with a knowing smile which reveals the fact that it will be as much good to you as an out-of-date railway timetable'.

What a host of rich characters were amongst the faithful who filled the pews Sunday by Sunday. There was the old lady I christened 'the prophetess Anna'—as she departed not from the temple night nor day and was always to be found pottering about doing the flowers. She had lived most of her life in the far east and I got used to her saying she was returning to her bungalow for tiffin, but when she referred to the verger as 'the church coolie' I felt that she was going too far!

When I first arrived we had a verger to whom the church was a constant surprise. If visitors asked about anything he would say: 'It's no good asking me, there are a lot of funny things go on in this place.' When I found him emptying any slops he had in the holy water stoups I felt he would be better employed elsewhere.

The enrolling member of the Mothers' Union was an enchanting Irishwoman whose heart was proportionate to her size. She is the only woman I have ever seen wearing gladioli on her corsage and the odd thing was they did not look out of place. She once arrived at church complaining of the fog, until it was pointed out to her that she had powdered her nose with her glasses on.

Another lady of great age, who wore hats piled with fruit, had in her youth been to confession to Dr. Pusey and worshipped on the highest pinnacles of Anglicanism ever since. She used to go to St. Paul's in the morning and St. Mary Magdalen's in the evening and someone said they could imagine her standing between Billy Favell and me singing: 'How happy could I be with either, were t'other sweet charmer away.' After Billy left Oxford she attached herself completely to St. Mary Magdalen's and gave me such large cheques at Easter that I blush to remember them.

Some of my flock provided problems such as the old lady who lived in a basement flat and thought people were stealing

157

her electricity so she kept all the plugs occupied with fires burning all over the floor amongst which she threaded her way in a flowing night-gown. I was so glad I didn't live in one of the flats above. When her bill came it provided her with yet further evidence that someone was tapping her electricity supply.

Close by lived a very grand old lady who had come to Oxford during the war with three maids, all dressed in caps with streamers, who had been with her ever since she was married many years before. She would not let them come with her to St. Mary Magdalen's saying: 'They wouldn't understand it, I think S. Philip & S. James is a much more suitable church for them.' I was touched that her last thought was that I should not be told of her death as I was away and she was afraid it would spoil my holiday. These are the sorts of things which more than counterbalance the disappointments and miseries one suffers in one's priestly life.

In 1951 I was elected as Guardian of the Shrine of Our Lady of Walsingham. This was a group of priests and laymen who acted as Trustees for the Norfolk Shrine which had been restored by Fr. Hope Patten who, like Noel Coward, was known amongst us as 'The Master'. He was something of an autocrat and used to having his own way. By the time I was elected there was beginning to be a new generation of Guardians who were not as content as their predecessors to rubber-stamp decisions which the Master had made without consultation.

This sometimes led to meetings of the Chapter which were fraught with tensions and I remember H.P., after a vote had gone against him, saying in an icy voice: 'When I brought the College of Guardians into being I thought that they would pay some attention to my wishes—I see that I was mistaken.' An uncomfortable silence ensued. However it was a closely knit and loyal group I joined and we were all personally devoted to H.P. so that when it came to the pinch we would bend over backwards to avoid doing anything that would really hurt him.

Roger Wodehouse was one of the Guardians and when going to Norfolk for Chapter I would pick him up at Brackley (for he always knew a convenient train to improbable stations) and we would motor via King's Lynn (where there was a special sort of bun he liked for tea). This love of trains and buns were two very dominant strains in his make-up.

Another Guardian was Fr. Raymond Raynes, Superior of the

158

Community of the Resurrection, to whom I became devoted for he had more sanctified common sense than anyone I have ever known. He came and conducted a Teaching Mission at St. Mary Magdalen's during which he kept me up talking half the night so that by the end of the week I felt as if I were walking in my sleep I was so tired. During those night vigils he told me wonderful stories of his battles with bishops and I particularly enjoyed his first meeting with the Bishop of Wakefield when he returned from South Africa to become Superior. The Bishop had hardly said 'How do you do' when he asked if his liturgical requirements were being observed in the chapel. This at once riled Fr. Raynes who replied coldly that as he had been away for ten years he had no idea what was being done. The Bishop then produced a wad of typescript from which he began to read while Fr. Raynes listened with growing impatience, and after a page or two he said: 'There's no need to go on, because from what I've heard I can tell you that these things are being done, but I can also tell you that speaking for myself and most of the community we find them extremely vexatious.'

The Bishop said smugly: 'They are my requirements for the whole diocese', and Fr. Raynes who was well roused by this time replied: 'I can't see what that has to do with our religious life. You may die tomorrow and then we shall probably have another crackpot with another set of ideas.' The Bishop rose saying: 'I'm not accustomed to being spoken to like this', but Fr. Raynes was not to be put down: 'If it comes to that, neither am I,' he replied 'I've spent the last ten years in a decent province of the Anglican Communion where we were governed by Synod and not by the whims of elderly eccentrics.'

This story was much in my mind when I saw the bishop in question, now retired and living in Oxford, standing at a North Oxford bus stop on a chilly morning. I had just been to bless the house of an old lady who said she had a poltergeist and there was a holy water bucket on the seat beside me. I wound down the window of my car and said: 'Can I give you a lift, Bishop?' 'Oh how kind', he said and opened the car door. What happened next was so swift that I really don't know how it could have occurred unless the poltergeist had got into the car, for the holy water bucket leaped off the seat straight at the bishop and covered him with holy water from head to foot.

I longed to tell Fr. Raynes how I had aspersed his old enemy, but it was just at this time he died and so I must wait to hear that rich laugh till we meet again in a land where bishops do not have liturgical requirements.

It was Fr. Raynes who was inadvertently responsible for the move which led to my leaving Oxford. The position of Registrar in the College of Guardians was vacant because one of the priest members holding that office had got married and there was a rule in the constitution that priests must be celibate. It was something about which H.P. was a fanatic and, although a majority of the Guardians did not agree with him, they felt it would be a reproach to bring his grey hairs in sorrow to the grave by changing anything he felt to be so important. Fr. Raynes then proposed that I should be the next Registrar and I protested feebly that I didn't really know what it involved. I was told that it amounted to being Vice-Chairman and if H.P. were to be ill I should have to take the chair in his place. What they did not tell me was that if he dropped dead I should have to carry on!

II

Walsingham

———————————

THE DEATH OF Fr. Hope Patten was as dramatic as anything he might have planned in his more theatrical moments. There was an episcopal pilgrimage taking place and an apostolic number of Guardians had gathered.

For some time he had been in bad health and often suffered what had become known as 'one of Father's turns', but he had all his life reacted badly to strain and worked himself to a stand-still so that those around him had come to regard these turns as 'the vapours'. It was a very hot, sultry August evening and after a heavy dinner we had a 'fervorino' in which the bishops, coped and mitred, were processed round the Shrine grounds singing 'Ave, Ave'—the mind boggles at the number of times H.P. must have sung those words during his thirty years at Walsingham— but he wasn't feeling like singing that evening. Having given Benediction and stepped out of sight of the congregation (he felt very strongly that a priest should not be seen at a disadvantage) he just collapsed and died shortly after from a heart attack surrounded by bishops and Guardians.

It was a great mercy of God that so many of us were there at the time for things simply went on without a break; if it had happened otherwise it would have been at least twenty-four hours before the Guardians could have assembled. As it was we could take decisions there and then and I discovered what being Registrar meant, for I had at once to take the lead. Much later one of the Guardians said to me: 'I suppose you know that when we elected you as Registrar we were conscious that we

F   161

were choosing H.P.'s successor?' I certainly did not know and if I had had a suspicion of this I should have been horrified.

I went to bed in the early hours of the morning with my mind in a turmoil, but even then it did not occur to me that this event was going to change my life completely. I was so entrenched in Oxford that I could not imagine myself ever moving and at that moment the church was closed for a complete remodelling of the chancel while we were using the chapel of Pusey House for services, which seemed no moment for me to be contemplating a move. Next morning the bishops suggested that they should just 'fade away', but I insisted they continue with their pilgrimage saying that if we couldn't cope with the death of the Administrator without shutting shop the sooner we closed down for good the better.

One of them said to me: 'You will have to come here and do this job, you know?' and I at once began to make excuse saying that I had recently been told by the doctor that if I did not ease up a bit on my present job I shouldn't last more than ten years. 'Ten years', the bishop replied, 'that's splendid! It's the next Lambeth Conference and we can have the whole thing over again.'

My immediate task was to arrange the funeral of H.P. and it proved to be a very moving sight, for we carried him from the Shrine to the Parish Church down the High Street which had seen so many festive processions, and most of the village followed the bier which was surrounded by Guardians. Two of the sacred ministers were village boys who owed their vocation to his influence and the third had lived as a layman in his Community of St. Augustine and was back acting as curate to the parish.

I never ceased to be impressed by the mark Fr. Patten had made upon this remote Norfolk parish. Someone who came to live there after his death and had not known him said to me: 'I've never heard anyone in the village speak of him without devotion and respect', and this is a county where the people are not backward in saying what they think about the clergy.

The Guardians elected me as Master of the College, but this still meant that we had to find an Administrator because, although H.P. had been both, the two offices were not necessarily synonymous. I could feel the noose tightening around my neck and I began to struggle against it.

I wrote around to several of the men's religious communities

162

hoping I might persuade them to take over the running of the Shrine, but none of them felt inclined to do so. I was very conditioned by H.P's thinking and felt that as a Holy Place it should be surrounded by 'monkery'. I believe if Fr. Raynes had still been Superior at Mirfield he would have used his influence to get the Resurrection Fathers to shoulder the responsibility; but he was already in his grave and there had been something of a reaction against his régime.

I had been in touch with the Bishop of Norwich and I arranged to go and see him. Here at last, I thought, was the bishop I had been waiting for since my birth with whom to do battle, for I felt sure he would be highly unreasonable. Secretly I hoped that we might have a resounding row which would give me a good excuse for keeping out of his diocese. In fact I found him a charming and sympathetic old man who wanted to do what he thought would be best for everyone. I was much touched when he said : 'Let's pray about it', and knelt down there and then on the carpet. He then declared himself quite certain that I ought to take over the job myself and promised that I should be properly licensed under seal and that it would be made quite clear that I was part of the diocese. As I drove back to Holt where I was staying with friends the seductive Norfolk landscape seemed to be playing its part in a conspiracy against me and I knew that my fate was sealed.

I saw the Bishop of Oxford and I said to him : 'I do try to be obedient sometimes, you know.' He replied : 'I'm sure you do, my dear Colin, and I don't think I've ever put you to the test. On the other hand it doesn't necessarily mean that silence gives consent !'

With a heavy heart I signed a deed of resignation in November and, as the pilgrimage season was over, arranged to move to Walsingham after the following Easter. The next five months were a prolonged agony of winding up my Oxford life, and I have never completely recovered from the emotional amputation which made the loss of my leg seem like a passing inconvenience.

One advantage of giving plenty of notice of my intention was that I was able to take an active hand in the appointment of my successor. No one now suggested that the church was redundant which was, at least, something accomplished in my ten years; but I was very anxious that the priest who followed me should be someone with an established position in the Catholic Movement. So many of the old stanchions who had kept the faith alive in Oxford had now died and been replaced with people like myself that I was certain the new Vicar of St. Mary Magdalen's ought to be a priest of considerable experience and standing.

Fr. John Hooper was a well-known figure in Anglo-Catholic circles although it would be hard to find a less 'party' man. It is his proud boast that he has never possessed a clerical collar. His appointment to St. Mary Magdalen was so right that it greatly eased my pains at leaving. The relationship of predecessor and successor is notoriously difficult and the fact that Fr. John and I have never experienced a moment of stress or strain is witness to his wonderful charity which is experienced by anyone who comes into contact with him.

The move to Walsingham was a nightmare. The removal men behaved like fiends. As it was the Easter holiday they began packing on Maundy Thursday although I was not leaving till the following Wednesday (which was All Fools Day). They got into my study while I was out and stowed away into the bottom of their cases all the things I had put on the top of my desk for immediate attention! I had some friends to luncheon and when the coffee came in so did three men in white coats who began packing the china, which brought my last party in Beaumont Street to a rapid conclusion. When I went to bed I discovered that the door to my bathroom was blocked by packing cases.

I set out for Walsingham in a new Bedford van which I had bought but never before driven, accompanied by my housekeeper and two friends who came to settle me in, and a couple of very disagreeable Siamese cats who much objected to being shut up in a rather smelly basket which the removers had produced. They kept up such continuous howls of protest that when we stopped for a picnic lunch we put them under a tree on the other side of the field where they were out of earshot.

On arrival at the College, Walsingham, the nightmare continued for it was something of a rabbit warren and I had no idea where my furniture ought to go. The men kept saying they couldn't get things in and leaving them out on the lawn. They did have the grace to look discomfited when they arrived to finish off next morning and found that the electrician and his mate, who were doing some rewiring, had moved it all in while we were at supper the night before.

The move seemed never to end for during the whole ten years I was at Walsingham there never appeared to be a time when we were not moving furniture from one end of the buildings to the other.

The College had been artfully contrived by Fr. Hope Patten out of rows of dilapidated cottages and had enormous charm but wild inconvenience. Each part had some separate heating unit which was very extravagant, laborious to operate and almost entirely inadequate. In fact the cats settled down more quickly than I did. On arrival they went to earth under a wardrobe, but next day made little voyages of exploration and would rush back to their refuge. Unfortunately we moved the wardrobe while they were out and put a chest of drawers in its place. The cats came dashing back and went full tilt into the bottom of the chest. They reeled back and fixed me with a look which would have stopped a bus.

When at last my furniture was arranged they recognised their claw marks and decided that this was home; something which I was never able to feel. One of the cats 'got religion' and would come dashing into church every time the Shrine bell rang. His sister never really took to it and would wait for him outside, her expression saying clearly: 'Those who go to church are no better than those who don't.'

I did not have much time to sit and mope for the pilgrimage season had begun and as I had no assistant there were a multitude of things to keep me busy, besides the time needed for finding my way around the labyrinth of customs which H.P. had woven about the Shrine. But at least I had not got the parish to worry about for I had made it clear that I felt the Shrine ought to be a separate thing. H.P. was talking of this at the time of his death and was preparing to resign as Vicar of Walsingham and remain as Administrator of the Shrine.

It is easy to see from the results that I made a mistake in following on this policy, but at the time I felt sure that it was the right thing to do and I cannot think how I should have managed that first summer when I was single-handed. And yet I cannot help feeling that if I had made a venture of faith someone would have come forward to help; for my experience has been that when a need arises at Walsingham it is always supplied and the right person comes at the right moment.

A vicar was appointed who did not much like having the

Shrine in his parish and found me difficult, so that the parishioners were faced with a problem of divided loyalties which in so small a place was an impossible situation.

I knew something about being a parish priest but the job I was taking on had so many ramifications and few of them were directly pastoral. To begin with I was responsible for maintaining the cult of Our Lady of Walsingham. Fr. Hope Patten had left the Shrine church filled with so many altars, images, reliquaries and vestments that it ought to have warmed the heart of even the most tepid ritualist. The trouble was that there was rather too much in too small a space and, while my life at St. Mary Magdalen had been dedicated to putting things in, at Walsingham I had to plan what could be taken out. Here lay the difficulty because there were those amongst H.P's female admirers who regarded the movement of a candle as treachery. 'Undoing Father's work', was a very favourite phrase and when I had a Sung Mass on S. Philip & S. James' Day one lady said: 'We never had Sung Mass in Father's day on Prayer Book Feasts.'

It was so different from anything I had experienced in Oxford and I found the squabbles behind the scenes hard to cope with. I began with the idea of getting those who worked for the Shrine into closer harmony, but the monthly discussions I tried to initiate seemed to increase the tensions and disagreements and so they were abandoned.

Although there was a capable Bursar I used to worry about the financial position which, at the time, was rather precarious; and largely through my fussing the Guardians decided to start a scheme of Planned Giving. It was a most dismal failure and we lost a lot of money in the venture. The interesting thing is that the moment we stopped the scheme money began to flow in and since then whenever we have needed to do anything—and we had to spend a lot during the time I was Administrator—the money has always been there.

I was Warden of the Children's Home and always felt that I had not enough time to give to the boys who needed all the attention and affection they could get. I did not seem to be very successful with them for after giving a serious talk to a boy who had taken money out of a box in the Shrine I cannot say that it had absolutely no effect, for he next robbed the Methodist Chapel!

There were so many departments for which the Administrator was ultimately responsible with the catering and billeting, a shop filled with hair-raising objects of piety and a home for old priests. The latter was still running when I took over, but with only two residents so that it was not the viable financial proposition it was supposed to be. The two residents could not have been more different. Fr. Tugwell, whom we called 'Tuggy', had been a monk on Caldy Island where he was known as Dom David. He had been sent off to Scotland to be ordained and for a long time I thought the Community had gone over to Rome while he was away and I could hear Tuggy grumbling: 'No one ever told me'—in the voice in which he often muttered to himself. However I later discovered that he had been recalled to the island and had made his own decision not to join the rest of the Community in submission to Rome. He was the priest who removed the Holy Sacrament from the monk's chapel and took it to the parish church. Oddly enough he did not join the remnant who started again to live the Benedictine life in the Church of England at Pershore Abbey, but became a secular priest although he had a simplicity and guilelessness which made him largely unable to cope with life outside a monastery.

When he left his last living of Hindringham, not far from Walsingham, he managed to burn the church registers while clearing out the Vicarage and had a sale in which he parted with a chest of drawers which had his false teeth in it. Nor did he think it in the least odd that a girl who had a crush on him should seize the Sunday joint, put it into her bicycle basket, and bring it to the Vicarage with her family pursuing on foot. He was most surprised when she was sent to hospital.

He settled in a room on the ground floor of the College with his cat, for which he would hide meat in his drawers and forget about it so that the stink became overpowering. At the same time he always threw any unwanted liquids out of his window into Knight's Street—as one passed the aroma became very like a back street in Naples. His only reading was the Breviary and the *Daily Express* both of which he would appear to be reciting with his lips slowly moving.

He was devoted to his old car which he treated like an animal often muttering at lunch: 'I think I'll take my car out for a little run this afternoon.' As he usually drove on the wrong side of the road those who went out with him said that it was as exciting as a trip on the Big Dipper. In the end it was worry over a slight accident with the car which caused his death. He asked me to read a statement he had drawn up for the insurance company and I felt bound to suggest that it would be better if he were to give one explanation and not three, each of which contradicted the other.

He never lost his monastic sense of obedience and would often explain things he did as being what the Abbot had told him to do; 'The Abbot' being Aelred Carlyle of Caldy. He was obedient to the last for the newest Deacon was with him as he lay dying and when the prayer 'Go forth Christian Soul' was said 'Tuggy' just heaved a great sigh and went forth.

His companion in the old priests' home was Fr. Panton, a retired priest of great rectitude and integrity who seemed to be taking refuge there from the female sex, for when his sisters came to see him during an illness he pulled the sheet over his face and pretended to be asleep, berating me afterwards for having let them in. A great female admirer went to see him when he was speechless after a stroke and was so moved that she kissed his hand.

She told me: 'I knew I had done the wrong thing, Father, because he growled at me.'

He was a naturally silent and reserved man, but had become more so since his stroke and growing deafness; but he would have his talking days when he would chat away without cessation. Those who had been at breakfast would report: 'Fr. Panton is having a talking day.' We were always fascinated by the fact that he appeared to need different spectacles for each course at a meal. Having sat down to the soup he would murmur apologetically: 'Wrong glasses', and go and fetch another pair which would be changed again when the meat was served.

After a bad heart attack when he turned quite blue, I came to anoint him and he said with some asperity: 'Opinions differ as to when unction is necessary but I suppose if you want to do it, you must.' He became very infirm and would often tumble about. Once a young man in the Shrine tried to steady him and he said in a voice of thunder: 'Unhand me, Sir,' his eyes starting out with indignation. At his funeral a rope broke and the coffin hurtled head first into the grave—I could almost see the look he would have given the undertaker.

The Guardians had somewhat twisted my arm to persuade me

to go to Walsingham and they were unfailingly kind and helpful, although as a Chapter we only met together twice a year so most of the time I was left to cope with crises on my own. The doyen was Fr. Fynes-Clinton, Vicar of St. Magnus-the-Martyr, London Bridge and from the earliest days a fervent and generous supporter of the Shrine. He always had come to Walsingham a lot but latterly he became very forgetful and would, as like as not, get on the wrong train and arrive at Harwich. He was the most charming, aristocratic and charitable man who although a great 'Papalist' was devoted to the Church of England so that it was inconceivable to those who knew him that he would ever change his allegiance.

I first set eyes on him when I was a boy. Having heard of this very 'extreme' church in the city of London I found my way to St. Magnus and discovered the Devotion of the Forty Hours in progress. A lot of old ladies, many wearing blue veils, were responding *'ora pro nobis'* to the Litany of the Saints. As I entered Fynes-Clinton had just said: *'Omnes sancti angeli et archangeli'*, and all the women shouted *'ora pro nobis'*. A reproachful face turned from the altar and said reprovingly, 'Orate *pro nobis'*.

I did not know him well till I became a Guardian, when we used to call him the 'Sergeant Major' as he would walk round telling us we were improperly dressed because the cords of our blue velvet mantles were not tied correctly. He sat next to Roger Wodehouse in choir and was so constantly telling him to stand up or sit down that it brought out the schoolboy in Roger who finally said 'Shan't' and remained seated.

There were those who treated Fynes as something of a joke, but he has never received recognition for two very valuable contributions he made to the life of the Church. He was among the first to begin having Masses at lunchtime for those who worked in the city and all the rich midday activity which now goes on in city churches owes much to Fynes' initiative. And at a time when to have friendly relations with Roman Catholics was regarded as disloyal Fynes went quietly on with his contacts and it was he who first invited the Abbé Couturier to come to England.

There was always a twinkle in those kindly old eyes and he had thoroughly enjoyed all the legal battles he had fought with protestants who had harried him when he first went to St. Magnus. Having fought and lost an order to remove six candle-

169

sticks from the high altar through various courts he took off the elegant set and replaced them by valueless wooden ones. He then made the complainants take them off with their own hands and sign a paper saying they had done so. This done he put back the original candlesticks and the objectors found that they had to start all proceedings again from the beginning and lost heart. He loved this sort of devious approach and at one time was contributing to something as the Revd. H. J. Fynes-Clinton for the benefit of the Vicar of St. Magnus-the-Martyr, which saved a lot of tax and which although quite legal we called jokingly 'the Clinton Swindle'.

As he became older he got more and more obsessed with the supernatural which had always fascinated him, and would tell how he had seen his grandfather in the restaurant car of an express train passing through Bletchley, adding: 'Of course he had been dead for years, it was a ghost train'; in the same tone of voice in which he might have said 'a goods train'.

He would often ask me with interest after I moved to Walsingham:

'Have you seen Patten yet?' and when I said 'No' would nod his head and say: 'Several people have, I believe.'

After a national pilgrimage at which there had been some protestant demonstrators he was making himself a cup of Horlicks in the college kitchen before going to bed and he remarked in a tone of real regret: 'Very quiet the Prots these days, usually when I appeared they used to sing "London Bridge is falling down".' This was the last visit he paid to the Shrine, but when he died I felt as if London Bridge *had* fallen down.

Another Guardian who was often at the Shrine was Sir William Milner, the giant baronet who had given the land on which the Shrine was built. When he came to stay we had to have a stool to extend the bed, but once he got into it he was very reluctant to leave it and I sometimes think that if there had not been Mass to get up for he would never have bothered to rise at all. He was a strange, lonely figure who had never had much family life as his mother died when he was young, his sisters were older than he and his father much taken up with public affairs, so that he was largely brought up by the butler. He felt that his great height separated him from other people and I got some idea of his loneliness when I stayed with him at Parcevall Hall, his lovely house in Wharfedale, where he had a private chapel with the Sacrament reserved. During the whole week-end not a single person called or rang up and if I had not been there he would have been entirely alone with the staff who bossed him unmercifully. (One could appreciate their point, for when staying at the College he was always late for meals and would then be prepared to sit at table half the afternoon.)

He once suggested that he should pay to have an extra door knocked through into our refectory from the room he normally occupied. As I knew this was to enable him to come to breakfast in a dressing gown I declined.

He was a sweet, gentle and very pious man, but maddening if one needed to get something done, for he had infinite powers of procrastination. He finally passed from this life leaving a wild confusion which could have been avoided if he had ever been prepared to put pen to paper except under extreme compulsion. All his large estate was left to be administered as the Walsingham Yorkshire Properties Ltd.

The first of the Guardians to die after I became Master was my old friend Roger Wodehouse. He came back from saying Mass, picked up *The Times* to read the Obituaries and fell forward dead. I remembered his saying to me years before: 'When I die I hope there'll be no nonsense about "No flowers and no mourning", I should like as much black and as many flowers as possible, mostly pink.'

John Upcott, a lay-Guardian who had been a housemaster at Eton died and left another sad gap, for how could one replace that salty and John Bullish figure who once said to me: 'I believe in treating boys unfairly, because life's unfair and the sooner they get used to the idea the better one is preparing them for life.' The first Christmas I was at Walsingham he sent me a case of sherry with a note saying that he had the feeling that I needed cheering up. He was carried to the grave by old boys of his house, many of whom he had jollied into the practice of the Catholic religion.

What rich characters most of the early Guardians were; and they began at this time to die like ripe apples falling from a tree, so that their hatchments on the wall of the Shrine soon numbered more than the living Guardians. Lord Norton died while on horseback at his home, Fillongley Hall near Coventry. His family had given much support to the Catholic Movement and he was related by marriage to the Birkbecks who had the same

171

background. He was so self-effacing and quiet that it took a little time to realise his immense strength of character and spiritual depth.

Much the same sort of person, but with a different background, was George Long, an original inhabitant of the village, who had been one of Hope Patten's earliest converts. He had been a churchwarden when the Guardians were founded and so made a member. He was quite prepared to clean the silver before the Guardians' dinner and undertake any menial task, but he was rich in a wisdom which only holiness can bring. Of course we elected others to fill their stalls, but the original Guardians really were the cornerstones upon which the true Shrine was built.

Perhaps the greatest difficulty I created for myself was the effort to establish some sort of community life at the College. This had been one of Hope Patten's dreams and till the time of his death he was still flogging a dead horse in the Community of St. Augustine which he had brought into being.

I had been ready enough to see the humorous side of this monastic experiment with its procession of unsuitable aspirants and claustromaniac sort of life. Yet I was sufficiently mesmerised by H.P's personality to feel that he was right in insisting that the Shrine must be surrounded by some form of religious life. The College had been constructed as a miniature monastery —there was even a Chapter House, with stalls and a lectern, made out of a former scullery—and to put it into use was an irresistible temptation to anyone with my background.

As I had been a Benedictine oblate for some years it seemed the best idea to try and establish a House of Oblates with the assistance of Nashdom and, as there was a former undergraduate who had lived with me in Oxford ready to be ordained and prepared to join the venture, I fell into the trap in which I found myself enmeshed for many years to come. At times it would seem as if we had achieved some sort of stability and it would then be broken by some member withdrawing and leaving us in confusion again.

Of course I was not really any good as a Superior as I found it difficult to be firm enough and was quite unable to deal with the petty feuds and jealousies which were always springing up. I often dreaded going home because of all the tiresome fracas which had arisen in my absence.

At last after being away in America for four months I returned to find things in considerable disarray and did what I ought to have done long before—packed up the whole venture.

I suppose we were, in our day, every bit as ridiculous as Hope Patten's canons, but there were good things about the life for the regular recital of much of the monastic office was an antidote to the large doses of extra-liturgical worship which we had to organise for the pilgrims—we would sometimes have Benediction four times in one day! Yet even the Divine Office became something of a burden for such a small number to maintain and on Saturday evenings, after the Pilgrimage Procession, when we settled down to recite Matins of the following day I would feel completely empty and exhausted.

We cared for some of the tiny surrounding parishes; they were a great joy and a wonderful contrast to the often over-pious pilgrims. I like to think that I was the last Rector of Stiffkey, as I looked after that parish for a year before it was absorbed into the Blakeney group. It was by tradition rather low church and they were not accustomed to vestments. However one Sunday I had been elsewhere and had brought no surplice with me so put on everything. Afterwards one of the congregation said: 'What beautiful robes you were wearing, Mr. Stephenson.' I replied: 'I've got a lot of these and you could have different ones every Sunday if you liked.' This was immediately passed around with excitement 'Mr. Stephenson says we could have different robes every Sunday', and after this I always wore vestments there without any further explanations.

Before I had been at Walsingham very long I had done an interregnum in most of the surrounding parishes and this, more than anything, broke down the local suspicion of the Shrine as being some different sort of religion. In many of the parishes the incumbents had been there as long as Hope Patten—the Rector of West Runton told me he had attended H.P's induction in 1921. The old Rector of Binham, an eccentric Irishman, usually wore a grey jacket over his cassock and a very old greening biretta squashed down on his head. In his rich Irish voice he once told us that his churchwarden had informed him on Sunday morning that the Diocesan Quota had been paid with some money he was keeping for something else and he ended: 'It quite spoilt the Holy Communion for me'—a phrase which, I fear, we adopted and used when something had irked us.

173

I find it sad that so many of these parishes have now lost their identity and have been lumped into groups—often the churches had been declared redundant. It is rather like Lord Beeching's solution for the railways and I suppose it is a realistic way of facing the problem of country churches with rising costs and fewer vocations to the priesthood, but I cannot help feeling that the church has lost its nerve and has not explored fully the possibility of part-time ministries and less drastic solutions. Always when a Church is to be closed there is a great outcry and one farmer who said, 'I am heart and soul in that church,' was told, rather tartly: 'It's a pity you aren't there physically a bit more.'

Before I came to Walsingham the great upheaval had begun in the Church at large. At St. Mary Magdalen we had started to have Evening Mass and I remember an old priest saying as he put on the vestments for the first time at that hour: 'Now I know how Harry Pollitt felt when the Communist line changed.'

The Reformation had caught up with the Roman Church, having been kept at bay for three hundred years, but it was bound to react upon the Church of England as always when the Roman Church has a cold the rest of us get pneumonia. Going over to Rome had become like jumping out of the fire into the frying pan.

I suppose Anglo-Catholics were hardest hit because we had always taken our stand on the fact that we were part of the Western Church and, as we thought the Church of Rome would never change, we ought to bring ourselves as far in line with it as we could. When Rome did change the ground was cut from under our feet and most of us were forced to think again, which is never a very comfortable exercise. Some just bashed on thinking they were marching ahead with a banner while all the time they were being left far behind. The Reverend Mother of one community said to me: 'Just as we are grateful to the Roman Church for having stood fast over some things, so they will be grateful to us for having stood fast over this.' The Community has already come to an end.

Others developed a curious position by demonstrating their devotion to the Church of England by continuing to do things which the Roman Church once did and had given up. The irony was that I had grown up thinking of Walsingham and all it stood for as the ultimate, but when I found myself in charge it had become obvious to me that unless it broke out of the rather restricted party circle with which it was associated the future was somewhat blank.

On the whole the pilgrims were very simple and uncomplicated souls. A young man, with a grant from the London School of Economics, did a survey on the type of person who came on pilgrimage and during one season we encouraged them to fill in a questionnaire. I don't know what his final findings were, but I looked at many of the forms before they were sent to him and to the first question: 'Are you Male or Female?' many had simply answered 'Yes'.

Whenever we had a big pilgrimage I usually got a crop of abusive letters one half complaining that too much of the Prayer Book had been used and the other half enraged because the Mass had not been Prayer Book enough. The trouble was that 'extreme' Anglo-Catholics had begun to feel insecure and this made them rather edgy and anxious that Walsingham should be a funk hole where only the élite could gain entry. The really disgruntled had always had an escape route by 'going over to Rome' and now they discovered the Roman Church doing all the things they most disapproved of in the Church of England. I was saddened that when it came to the point Anglo-Catholics could display exactly the same sort of intolerance and lack of charity which I had always associated with extreme protestant groups.

Yet most memories of Walsingham are happy despite the many frustrations of trying to get the different departments all working smoothly at the same time. I am convinced that the power of evil is always very active at a particularly holy place and I never ceased to be amazed at patterns of behaviour which seemed almost like devil possession. I well remember a whole series of events which led up to an evening when the Vicar was away and I was in charge of the parish and the beautiful medieval church of St. Mary, where the revival of the Shrine had begun, was burned to the ground. The origin of the fire is mysterious and was probably due to an electrical fault in the organ; yet there was a curious atmosphere of evil at the time to which the fire seemed to act as a catharsis. The mighty roof groaned like a lost soul as it fell into the inferno of flame. On the previous afternoon I had been in the church to hear confessions and I had seen a young man wandering around. He was about the same

175

age as I had been when I had paid my first visit and I could not help wondering if it was making something of the same impact on him it had made on me thirty years before. By the morning it had ceased to exist and that particular manifestation of H.P's genius had been completely rubbed out.

If the power of evil sometimes made itself felt, it was negligible compared with the power of good of which one was constantly aware; for even not very sensitive people are conscious of the atmosphere of Walsingham. I could tell many tales of those converted from unbelief, instantly like St. Paul, and others healed mysteriously by the water of the Holy Well.

To live alongside this kind of experience involves a great emotional expenditure and I, and those who worked with me, felt completely drained at the end of a pilgrimage season. But I endured nothing of the strain H.P. had suffered because I had only kindness and understanding from the diocesan authorities. In my first year the Bishop of Thetford, who was son of the old priest with whom I had first walked the Walsingham Way, came to the national pilgrimage, which was the first official recognition which the Shrine had received.

The diocesan, Lancelot Fleming, was unfailingly kind and sympathetic and invested me with astounding respectability by making me a Canon. I was also elected by the clergy of the diocese as a Proctor in Convocation, which was another sign showing that Walsingham was accepted in the diocese and that I had accomplished something of what I set out to do. I cannot say that I much enjoyed the wrangles about prayer for the dead and Anglican-Methodist reunion which went on in Church House. I saw the point of the answer made by Ronald Knox to someone who remarked on the fact that he had never been to Rome since he became a convert. He replied: 'If you are liable to suffer from sea-sickness it is very unwise to go too near the engine room.' I found the Church of England's engine room made me very queasy.

In 1965 I had been a priest for twenty-five years, which I found very hard to believe, and I had a little celebration during which I sang Mass for the first time facing the people at a portable altar we had placed in the sanctuary of the Shrine church and which has been in use ever since. I could not help reflecting how much the ceremonial surrounding the Mass had changed since I first approached the baroque high altar of SS.

Mary & John twenty-five years earlier.

When I first sat down after the Communion, when saying Mass for the Sisters, in order to make the short pause for meditation suggested at that moment, the dear things brought me a cup of tea afterwards thinking I had been taken ill. But the 'wind of change' was also sweeping through the religious orders and the Sisters at Walsingham soon 'changed their habits' in every sense. They were a wonderful help and support from the first moment of my arrival and I never ceased to be amazed at the way in which Mother Margaret could be faced with some ghastly imposition and simply say: 'That will be lovely, Father' —and mean it!

One morning I was driving her back to Walsingham in my Bedford van as we had been early to Norwich where a Sister was having an operation. I had been home about half-an-hour when two policemen, straight from 'Z Cars', appeared and asked me if I was the owner of the Bedford van outside and if I had been driving from Norwich to Fakenham that morning! I was horrified thinking I must have knocked someone over, but they said a report had come in that a van with this number had driven through Drayton with a woman in the back with a sack over her head, tied up and screaming. They made it clear that they were very suspicious of the whole place when I took them up to the Convent, peering at the many doors and passages. It was obvious how they thought we got hold of nuns, and they asked the Reverend Mother if we had been alone. When they left they said: 'We are sorry to have bothered you, Madam.' Mother Margaret replied sweetly: 'Not at all, if I had been tied up I should have been most grateful to you for coming so quickly.' After they had gone the local policeman rang up to apologise and said: 'They have only just come to the district, if they'd come to see me first you'd never have been troubled.'

My own Mother died in Hove after a short illness, but she had become very forgetful for some time and although she always said that she went to Mass on Sunday she had ceased to know one day of the week from another. A local clergyman had called on her and as he left he said: 'I fear our simple services would not be to your taste, Mrs. Stephenson.' My mother said to me ingenuously: 'I can't think what made him say that.' I pointed out that her flat was rather full of photographs of me in a biretta and clutching rosaries.

177

I was lucky enough to reach her in time and to be able to give her the Last Sacraments while she was conscious and knew me. As I sat beside her while she was dying I read *Soundings*, the essays of rather 'mod-theology' by Cambridge theologians which had just been published. It put many of the things they were fussing about in their right perspective to be with someone about to face the ultimate reality.

When I buried her in the churchyard at Henfield it was midday and a bell was ringing from Cowfold Monastery over the fields. It brought back in a dramatic way so many childhood memories and the mystified look on her face when I said I had been at the monastery which, now I know more of the world, I realise was combined with an anxiety of what I had really been up to. At least parents didn't have to worry about drugs in those days!

The death of one's mother is bound to be something of a traumatic experience because she is the only person who knew you before you were born. Mine often said to me: 'Wait till you're my age, and you'll see things differently', and as I get older I understand what she meant.

Relentlessly the pilgrims came and went, being replaced immediately by others and I realised what H.P. had meant when he spoke of 'the grind of Walsingham'. I travelled far more widely than he had been able to do and went twice to America to talk about the Shrine, but it was a great strain, and always when I returned there was an infinity of problems awaiting my attention.

Every year the numbers increased and the season got longer. It was essential to build a new pilgrim refectory and provide more accommodation in the Hospice, particularly for sick and disabled pilgrims. Of course this meant destroying some of the rather charming features of the old pilgrimage pattern with the attractive barn refectory and quaint old rooms which I had known and loved when I first stayed in the Hospice as a boy. The truth was that we were moving out of the amateur into the professional league; and I was lucky to have on my staff a priest who had some knowledge and skill in architecture and who was able to lift some of the bricks-and-mortar worries off my shoulders.

I could hardly believe that the end of my tenth year at Walsingham was approaching. I have always felt that it is better to leave a job while it is in a flourishing condition rather than wait for signs of recession and I am inclined to think that in ten years you have given a job all that you have to give.

I spoke to the Guardians about this in Chapter and they were somewhat dismayed at the thought of change, but kind and sympathetic. I had not the least idea of what God wanted me to do and for the first time since I became a priest I felt confused. For some time I had been in a great state of tension and would wake in the morning full of apprehension without the least idea what I was worried about.

Then God spoke quite clearly and unequivocally for I had a slight coronary thrombosis. All the worry and tension went, but I knew without a shadow of doubt that my work as Administrator at Walsingham was done.

12

Hims Ancient and Modern

As I LOOK BACK over my life I am fully conscious that I have managed to create my own 'Anglican attitude' and hold it against all intrusion of reality.

Once in Oxford the Evangelical newsagent gave me the *Church of England Newspaper* in mistake for the *Church Times*. His apologies were rather overdone and he revealed that his vicar had told him St. Mary Magdalen was nothing to do with the Church of England. I at once became rather haughty and said: 'On the contrary, we *are* the Church of England.'

It was easy in Brighton to see only one side of the coin, for the Anglo-Catholic churches were big, aggressive and, in my youth, very flourishing. In Oxford it was very easy to restrict my interest in the same way, for naturally the Movement which bears the name of this city had left its mark on the churches. I did once go into a low church and the clergyman who was standing at the door said: 'Dull, isn't it?' I agreed heartily till I discovered he was talking about the weather!

At Chichester Theological College I was in a community where we all had much the same outlook and we thought moderate and low Anglicanism very funny. I can, however, quite see that Catholic ceremonial appears slightly hilarious to those who are not accustomed to it—a naval friend visiting St. Mary Magdalen's said: 'When all those bells went off I thought it was Action Stations.' Now that things have changed I can appreciate that all that bobbing up and down must have seemed very peculiar. Yet I sometimes wonder if the low

180

church clergy realise that what they do seems just as comic to those not brought up in that tradition.

As a curate in Cowley St. John I worked in a completely monochrome district as far as the church was concerned which with its convents and schools was very self-contained but hardly representative of the church as a whole. In the Navy I took my own religion around with me and through the kindness and tolerance of those I served as chaplain I was able to establish my own version of the Church of England wherever I went. During my time in hospital I was more vulnerable but, except for my brief spells in the Wingfield Hospital, such ministrations as were available were more or less in the tradition that I understood.

St. Mary Magdalen, Oxford was a congregation rather than a parish in the accepted sense and was in some ways what I liked to make it. To flourish in a place like Oxford a church must have a definite colour and I made it very definite. Perhaps the tragedy of Oxford is that there is no lively church which provides 'middle-stump' Anglicanism so that the undergraduate who wishes to worship outside his college chapel must choose between 'incense' or 'the north end'. Once, giving a gentle pull to the leg of the Vicar of St. Aldate's, who had taken me to see the redecoration of his church, I said : 'I don't like that second holy table, that's where the rot begins. If you want to see what it leads to take a look inside my church.'

Walsingham was perhaps the greatest flight from reality of all for it was designed by a genius to give the impression that the Reformation had never happened and that the Church of England was indistinguishable from the Roman Church. By the time I went there I was a less dedicated 'party man' than I had been for most of my life; but there were two experiences, more than any other, which made me see the Middle Ages and the Church of Rome in a different light so that I was not prepared to bury my head in the Walsingham sand.

The first was that on two visits to Mount Athos in Greece I found the life and thought of the Middle Ages still going on, having continued without change from the fall of Constantinople, and so I was able to study it in action. The second experience was a private audience with Pope John XXIII which gave me a new vision of the Roman Catholic Church.

The Holy Mountain of Athos is situated at the end of a

peninsula which juts out to sea at the top east side of Greece. It is cut off by forests and mountains and so has always been difficult of access from the land. There are many legends of its origin as a monastic centre. It is said to be the Mount of Temptation to which the devil took Our Lord to show him all the kingdoms of the earth. Some of the monks claim that God put hermits there with his own hand to see if human beings could live the life of angels.

It would seem that, as in the Arabian deserts, Christians sought solitude here from fairly early times and gradually formed themselves into communities, but anchorites have always lived in the caves on the eastern tip of the peninsular, and still do so today. It became a complete monastic kingdom and it is still claimed that no woman's foot has ever been set on the Holy Mountain and this prohibition extends also to all female animals. This, alas, does not seem to include fleas and bugs which breed in plenty, also one hears a suspicious clucking of hens around some of the more relaxed establishments!

Gradually there developed twenty monasteries, a large number of hermits and little monastic housing estates where they live together in twos and threes with a central church, to which they all go on Sundays and feasts. These last establishments are known as *Sketes*.

Athos has always been under the jurisdiction of the Patriarch of Constantinople, but there was a Latin Monastery there till after the Great Schism. During the fourth crusade an attack was made on the Holy Mountain and several of the monks were burned as heretics—an outrage which has left its mark to this day in a hatred and suspicion of anything Latin.

At the time of the Fall of Constantinople the monks made a separate peace with the Turks, and were left more or less undisturbed and allowed to govern themselves, except that a Turkish pasha took up residence at Karyes, the monastic capital, where he existed in an enforced exile from his harem. The religious life went on as it had always done and Athos became the last outpost of Byzantium as it remains today.

I first read about the Holy Mountain in a somewhat scabrous and unfair book called *The 5000 Beards of Athos;* but it had wonderful photographs which quickened my imagination and aroused a longing to go there. I had come in contact with the Orthodox church while an undergraduate at Oxford, through

182

the Fellowship of St. Alban & St. Sergius, an association of Anglicans and Orthodox; and I attended one of the pre-war conferences of the Fellowship which were held at High Leigh in Hertfordshire where impressive bearded figures from the Continent mingled with sober Anglican bishops, who kissed icons and did all manner of exotic things at variance with the restraint they exhibited in their own dioceses. I airily asked an Orthodox monk there to bless an icon I had bought. I thought he looked a little shaken and discovered he had got no Holy Water with him and the rite of consecration takes several hours. He returned it to me next morning having been up half the night.

When I was Vicar of St. Mary Magdalen, Oxford, for some time the Orthodox had their Liturgy in the church—in theory after we had finished—but the priest started earlier and earlier so that those attending Mass in the Lady Chapel found themselves at an entirely different service, while the mutterings and clanking of censer chains made it reminiscent of the Church of the Holy Sepulchre while I was trying to preach.

I shall never forget my first sight of Athos early on a May morning. We had experienced an exciting drive down the peninsular for the civil war was barely finished and all the bridges were down. We had stayed the night in an ancient haunted tower as the guests of a remarkable pair of English Quakers who had lived in this isolated spot since the end of the Great War. Hermits came down to them from their caves from time to time to get vitamin pills—which is a service the Desert Fathers never had within reach. Before dawn broke we got a fishing boat and as the sun rose we sailed along the south coast of Athos and began to see the picturesque buildings, every one of which had a small dome on some part of it which was the chapel as they were all occupied by monks.

Soon we saw the first of the monasteries and then the simply vast buildings of St. Pantelamon, the Russian Monastery, which once had over a thousand monks, but since the Revolution has dwindled in number till only a handful of old men with white beards keep the chant going in their enormous church.

It was the Orthodox Holy Week and we arrived at the Monastery of Dionysiou on Good Friday. I had gone ahead as my companion went to Karyes to present our credentials to the Holy Synod. He had taught me to say: 'I am an English priest'

183

in Greek, but when I got there I apparently said 'I am the English Pope'—which caused quite a stir!

Dionysiou is built high on the rocks above the sea with crazy wooden balconies poised dangerously over space. It would be hard to imagine anywhere more romantic in appearance and I have always thought we were very lucky in our choice of the first monastery we visited, for although I have since been to almost all of them, I never discovered another where the abbot and monks were so simple and friendly nor the observance so good. The Guest House being full for the Easter Festival I was given a cell amongst the monks and so felt very much part of the community.

As the monks still keep to Byzantine time, which counts sunset as midnight, I soon lost all sense of day and night and through the long Easter services during which I stood propped in a stall with a candle in my hand, I constantly found myself dropping off to sleep and waking just in time to tighten my grip on the candle before it got to the lighted end. After four hours in church I was led to my cell by a monk who said: 'Now we will repose for an hour and then we will go to church.'

I wore a cassock and a biretta for if one is a priest one would feel very naked without something to cover one's head, surrounded as one is by monks who put a veil over their stove pipe hats when they go into church. They are supposed never to cut their beards or their hair which they wear in a bun and literally 'let down their hair' for the Anaphora. There are no mirrors on the Holy Mountain, but the more vain do quite well gazing into still water as they do their hair. I found one poor little monk who could hardly produce any hair at all on his face and at his earnest pleas I sent him a bottle of very old fashioned hair restorer which had very encouraging pictures on the label.

They have clung to their traditions with a wonderful tenacity and even many of the sanitary arrangements are medieval. I could write a whole thesis on the strange and noisesome closets to be encountered in this monastic kingdom.

The monasteries were rich in treasures of manuscripts, paintings, icons and reliquaries mostly of the Byzantine period but what chiefly fascinated me was that here was the Middle Ages, to which I had always looked with such romantic nostalgia, still in action. It was possible to see very clearly both its strength and its weakness.

The worship is rich and wonderful. One prays that the Orthodox church never has the sort of Reformation which has taken so much of the mystery and symbolism out of the churches of the west. Yet their outlook has got strangely divorced from normal life and many of the monks were very lazy fellows who spend a lot of their time just sitting around, for eastern spirituality has tended to regard monks as primarily 'praying machines'. There has never been the tradition of 'scholar monks' which we have had in the west. We were told all over Athos with great awe of a monk at the Grand Lavra who was writing a book. When we met him we found he was keeping a scrap book and pasting in photographs from *Picture Post*.

On my first visit I was much taken with the oddities of the monks I met, it was only when I returned that I began to realise that those who are most anxious to speak with visitors are not the most admirable examples and that behind them are a lot of really saintly and disciplined men. But there has been a division amongst the monasteries and about half have thrown over the rule of a single abbot, community of property and communal feeding. They call themselves Ideorhythmic (which means everyone following their own rhythm), the rich monks pay the poorer ones to wait on them and live in very comfortable apartments, while the ancient and splendid refectories stand empty. It is very much monasticism in decline and it is significant that they have shrunk in numbers far more drastically than the older form of cenobitic monastery. In them one could see the sort of situation which led to the dissolution of the monasteries in England.

I don't suppose one would find anyone on Athos prepared to debate how many angels can sit on the head of a pin, but many of their theological preoccupations are of that order and their intolerance has to be seen to be believed. Their old beards tremble and their eyes flash at the very thought of what they regard as heresy. Time has stood still and when they speak of something it is often hard to gather whether it took place three, thirty or three hundred years ago.

I was told of a visitor who was taken illegally by a monk to the charnel house at Dionysiou and stole the skull of a holy monk who had not been long dead (for they are buried in lime and their bones dug up a few years later). An anchorite who had lived in a cave below the monastery for some time saw in a vision the skull being taken and left his cave at once and told the abbot. He set off in pursuit of the visitor and regained the skull, while the monk who had broken the rules by taking someone to the charnel house was severely punished. This event, which comes straight out of the Middle Ages, had, I discovered, happened the year before I was told of it.

Athos is a wonderful place and I should hate it to be thought that I have anything but veneration for its monks and gratitude for the kindness they showed me during my visits, but it did reveal to me very clearly the dangers of trying to shut the Church up in the past. So much of the Catholic Movement in the Church of England has been a turning backwards and a holding on to certain positions with a fanaticism bred from a sense of insecurity. I realised that while I should never find the Reformation attractive, yet the Reformers had a point, faced with the situation they found; and their valid insights into the living of the Gospel have been enshrined in bodies which we have rather contemptuously called 'dissenting'.

Every period in the history of the Church has much to teach us and there are many things, the crusades for one, of which we should be heartily ashamed; but our duty is to live in the Church today which involves situations which cannot be met by a slavish imitation of the past be it Puritan, Catholic or Primitive. This is particularly true of liturgy. Series 2 and Series 3 will soon be as much amongst the fossilised relics as 1662 and 1928. I am glad that I live in the Church now for, in spite of its absurdities, I am conscious of the Holy Spirit at work.

The second experience happened in February 1961 when a brief notice appeared in the *Observatore Romano* recording that I had had a private audience with the Pope and speculating that I had been sent as an emissary of the newly elected Archbishop of Canterbury. This attracted the attention of the English press and I was rung up by several reporters to whom I acknowledged that I had indeed had an audience with Pope John, but that it was as a private individual and I had no comment to make.

It happened in this way : while at Walsingham I used to take my holiday in the winter and I was staying in Rome for several weeks. I had been given introductions to a variety of ecclesiastics so that I was soon bustling in and out of the Vatican as if it were a club. I saw the Pope when I attended the very private 'giving of the biretta' on the evening before the American Bishop of St. Louis received his Cardinal's hat at a Consistory in St. Peter's. At the latter ceremony I was given a ticket for the diplomatic box close to the Pope's throne and was able to observe the skill with which the Master of Ceremonies dealt with the aged cardinals' long scarlet trains, preventing them from falling flat on their faces as they descended the steps after having given their homage to the Holy Father. I had a perfect view of Pope John who presided like a very kindly old nanny who has got the children into the nursery and is delighted by their good behaviour.

A few days later I was rung up at my pensione by a Monsignor, who had been most kind and attentive to me since my arrival, and he said: 'I've told the Holy Father you're here and he's very anxious to see you if you can spare the time. He's rather taken up with the cardinals at the moment, but once they've gone he hopes you can have a long visit with him.' I was rendered almost speechless with surprise, but managed to stammer a few words of grateful appreciation and delight.

Next day a very impressive letter was delivered by a Papal messenger. It was an official summons to an audience with the Holy Father and my shares rose considerably with the staff of the simple pensione at the top of the Spanish Steps where I was staying.

I dressed myself in a black suit with clerical collar and, taking as much literature about Walsingham as I could collect, I presented myself at the Vatican where I made contact with my Monsignor friend who was to present me. We went down to the Papal apartments in a lift with gilt baroque fittings which seemed big enough to hold a small-sized sherry party.

I had never before realised that the Papacy is in fact a Renaissance Court and is still carried on with much of its splendour. All that morning the Pope had been receiving cardinals in audience and so everything was in full flower. We passed through room after room filled with decorative figures in elaborate uniforms, Swiss Guards, Civil Guards, Gentlemen-in-Waiting, Noblemen of the Holy See and Papal Chaplains, all standing about doing nothing in particular.

I was getting a little anxious about details of protocol and asked what I ought to do on meeting the Pope. The Monsignor said: 'We are supposed to genuflect three times as we approach the Holy Father, but you won't be expected to do that!' I replied that I would wish to do whatever showed proper respect; but he was quite right for I had no sooner entered the library and gone down on one knee than the Pope pounced upon me, pulling me to my feet in a great bear hug and saying, in English: 'Get up, get up.'

It was symbolic of the difference between him and his predecessor that the desk used to be at the far end of the long room so that visitors had to approach under the close scrutiny of mesmeric eyes, but Pope John immediately had his desk moved just inside the door. He led me to a chair and sat beside me talking while the Monsignor translated: 'The Holy Father says that he understands perfectly your position as an Anglican priest but he wishes you to remember that you are already united with him in believing in Our Lord and Our Lady, the Church and the Sacraments. These are important things and the matters which divide you are just not important.' Meanwhile the old man was looking at me fixedly to observe my reactions and was nodding and smiling.

I was, of course, amazed for this line of Pope John, which became the theme of much of his ecumenical thinking, was at that time quite new to me. When I remembered the heart-searchings which many of my friends had endured before deciding that they could no longer remain in the Church of England it seemed almost incredible that this kindly old man, wearing the great gold Fisherman's ring, and who in the claims made about his jurisdiction represented one of the greatest problems, could be talking in this way.

There was a warmth and joyousness which seemed to flow from him and I felt at once that he was a very loving man who longed to give pleasure and happiness to everyone and that to him charity overruled everything, making him speak with a divine disregard for theological niceties.

In the absurd way in which my mind flits off at tangents I could not help being fascinated by the immaculate whiteness of his cassock wondering if he put on a clean one every day.

I obviously had the whole of his attention and already his fertile mind was weaving a little fantasy to bring the conversation round to what he wanted to talk about. He said that he had been thinking about my name before I had come to see him and it had occurred to him that St. Stephen had known Our Blessed Lady so that it was appropriate that a son of St. Stephen should be in charge of one of her Shrines. This led me to talk about Walsingham, which is what Pope John wanted to hear about and he listened with fixed attention, every now and then asking some question which showed that he was taking a real interest in everything I was telling him. I produced the pictures of the Shrine I had brought with me and he looked at them closely putting on his spectacles to do so and saying several times 'Bella! Bella!'

I told him of the difficulties Fr. Hope Patten had experienced in the early days of the restoration and of the Bishop of Norwich's objection to the stone let into the wall of the Holy House recording that it had been built 'when Pius XI was Pope, Bertram, Bishop of Norwich and Hope Patten, parish Priest of Walsingham.' When I got to the climax of the story, that the final solution had been to obliterate the Bishop's name and leave in the Pope's, John XXIII threw back his head and roared with uninhibited laughter.

Becoming serious again he said that he was glad that the Pope's name should appear in the Anglican Shrine as it showed that, in spite of the unhappy division, the Church of England was part of Western Christendom. He then went on to say that he felt sure that the common devotion to the Mother of the Lord we both acknowledged would draw us closer together in Christ. As he spoke of Our Lady he looked affectionately at an exquisite enamel of Mary framed in gold which was on his desk, much as anyone might look at the photograph of a beloved parent or friend. It was so simple and artless having nothing affected or dramatic about it and it told me more about his personal devotion to Our Lady than any theological discourse could possibly have done.

He began to ask questions such as if we expected the pilgrims to make their confessions and how we managed the finances. He nodded his head with approval as my replies were translated to him and I explained in some detail how the Shrine was staffed and organised.

He asked me if I was married and when I said I was not he stretched out a hand and patted me on the back saying that he was sure celibacy was the better way for a priest and that there must always be some who were prepared to make the sacrifice.

Asking if I enjoyed good health, he said: 'I too keep very well. I come from a long-lived family and I think I'm going to surprise a lot of people.' This was at the beginning of his reign when it was being said quite openly that he had been put in as a 'caretaker' Pope. He did indeed surprise a lot of people but he did it in a very short time.

He made a little joke which he was fond of making to Anglicans. He said: 'I am no longer the "prisoner of the Vatican", but it really amounts to that because I can't go where I would like to and so sometimes the time hangs rather heavily on my hands and this is particularly so in the evenings. So I sit at the window with my binoculars trying to pick out the churches and I see a little white spire and I know that's All Saints English church. So you see I keep my eye on you constantly.'

I had been with him for almost three-quarters of an hour when he opened the drawers of his desk and gave me a splendid bronze medal of himself in a small case, apologising that it was not of more precious metal. He then began to give me piles of medals and rosaries, which he had blessed, for me to distribute amongst my friends so that I said I felt like the Children of Israel spoiling the Egyptians which made him laugh.

With extraordinary sensitivity he said: 'I must find some white rosaries for your Sisters, now tell me their names', and he counted the sets of beads out one by one repeating the names of the Sisters as I told him. It was an act of imaginative charity to send a personal greeting to nuns of another communion in this graceful way.

The fun behind his sparkling eyes was never long in bubbling to the surface and when I knelt for his blessing he said: 'My word, what a big man you are! It will take me all my time to fill you up with blessings.'

I said: 'May I take your blessing to those who work for the Anglican Shrine?' and he replied, choosing his words very carefully: 'I would wish my blessing to descend on all who visit your Shrine', then after a pause he added: 'Not as exerting authority, but in all charity', and he repeated 'in all charity' three times.

Before I left he told me that he would offer his Mass and Offices for me and my work on the following day and hoped I would write to him, but he said: 'Send it under cover to the

Monsignor and he will put it into my hand. If you send it in any other way heaven alone knows where it will end up.'

I retraced my steps through the ante-rooms in a state of euphoria. It was pouring with rain outside and I was given a lift away from the Vatican by an American bishop, now a cardinal, who was sitting in the back of an enormous car dressed in a beaver hat and purple feriola, as he had had an audience with the Holy Father that morning. As I climbed in beside him he gave me a nudge and said: 'You see I've gone native today!' As we drove through the crowded lunch-time traffic we talked about our audiences and the man to whom we had been speaking. When I left him he said: 'You may think, Father, that it would be difficult to regularise your position, but I know this guy: if he means to have a thing, he'll have it.'

I thought of this many times as Pope John's idea for a Vatican Council was pushed gently but firmly forward and the great Roman Church, so monolithic, began its agonising process of self-reformation.

An R.C. bishop speaking to Anglicans at Walsingham said: 'You must remember that we have been brought up on the idea of "the blood of the martyrs" and "the conversion of England" and although we may now see with our minds that this is a rather limited outlook we shall go on reacting emotionally in this way for some time; so you must try to be patient with us because we're doing our best.'

When I took a party on pilgrimage to Lourdes and found that throughout France we were given the hospitality of altars while at Lourdes itself we were treated as members of the family I realised that Pope John was not just an elderly idealist enchained by a medieval system but a very holy old man who had grasped the simple fact that love was the heart of the Christian gospel and the only weapon that any follower of Christ had any right to use. The reformation in the Roman Church made me see the sixteenth century upheavals in a new light and to have a far greater sympathy with the reformers.

I deplore the modern iconoclasm as much as I do that of an earlier age—at one church in France they made a bonfire on the church steps of the old fiddle-back chasubles and Latin missals—but who am I to speak who have always claimed that I could not bear moderation? I understand why the young react against ecclesiasticism and some of the man-made structures of the Church as very unlovely things, and yet I don't think they realise what fun we had while it lasted!

In a book like this it would be so much tidier if I could die at the end so that I might complete the picture, but I believe that the Holy Spirit is a living power and that he will change my reactions and ideas, not only in this life, but far more drastically in the life to come.

Perhaps I will manage to continue to live all my life as an Anglican in a fantasy world, for I now spend much of my time acting as chaplain to friends who have a large house, a chapel where the Holy Sacrament is reserved, and where we are surrounded by many people of 'like mind', and this is perhaps as untypical of the Church of England as any of the other experiences I have had.

I do not now believe there was ever any hope of converting the Church of England as a whole to baroque Catholicism, but I am glad to have lived at a time when for a moment it seemed a dizzy possibility. I am glad that I experienced something of the splendour of its worship and the tortuous complexities of its disciplines and never for a moment do I regret the day on which I first pushed open the door of St. Bartholomew's, Brighton and there and then formed an attitude to Anglicanism to which I shall react emotionally till the day of my death.

CPSIA information can be obtained
at www.ICGtesting.com
Printed in the USA
LVHW081427100721
692024LV00008B/68